Wake Up Call From Houston

Will Americans Heed the Wake-Up Call from Houston?

Speaking via telephone from Houston, Texas on Tuesday morning, August 29, LaRouche PAC Policy Committee member Kesha Rogers reported the following:

"I'm standing right here in a grocery store. You look at the conditions... Now they're talking about how the water supply in the Houston area might be compromised; we don't know how far that goes or how serious it is going to get, but you have lines in the grocery store that are back out the door and wrapped around the grocery store building, with hundreds of people waiting to buy groceries, to buy food, because they have been out of food supplies for a very long time. I was standing in line, talking to people who have lost their homes, lost everything—they had water in their houses coming all the way up to their chests— and these were people who were able to get out with family members, who were rescued and taken to other locations.

"In talking to some of these people on the ground here about this situation, what is obvious is that this is not going to be a 'quick fix' here—this is not just about infrastructure breakdown, but you've got tens of thousands of people who have just lost everything. It makes the point very clear how important it is that our solution, including Glass-Steagall—the economic recovery program that Lyndon LaRouche has put on the table— cannot be just a piece of legislation that people get to when they get to it. I don't think you can simply say 'It's going to cost $300 billion or $200 billion,' or whatever number they're putting out. It really has to be a federal credit program, to do everything that has to be done to put people back into living conditions, such that they can have homes and have a life again. This is not

about how much insurance policy was lost... The main thing is that this is a wake-up call. We're going to have a lot of leadership to provide, a lot of work to do, not just to build up this state, but to use this as an opportunity to build up the nation."

We Must Measure Up to the Challenge

The world is watching the devastation in Houston, and the American people are watching. Some are responding with volunteer labor, with donations, and with other charitable actions. But what have the American people done to prevent such disasters? Houston is notoriously unprepared to deal with flooding even during annual storms, let alone hurricanes or the current 1,000-year flood. Already in 2012,— five years ago— the American Society of Civil Engineers gave the city a C-minus on its "report card" regarding flood control. The two primary flood control dams for Houston, both on the verge of overflow or even collapse in the current storm, were built in the 1940s, and are twenty years past their life expectancy.

Houston is no different from essentially every part of these United States. Our greatest city, New York, is undergoing a general breakdown in transportation, sanitation, water, and more—a reality addressed on Aug. 26 at a LaRouche PAC forum in Manhattan. The infrastructure deficit has created powder-kegs across the nation, only needing a spark to set them off, as we saw with Hurricane Katrina in New Orleans, with superstorm Sandy in New York City, and with the drought in the Southwest.

American infrastructure is collapsing, and has been for years. As emphasized by Kesha Rogers, the issue is not about dollars and cents, but about human lives, and the futures of millions of families who are now suffering or at risk. We, as a nation, have sat by and let this disastrous situation come to this point.

China and Hamilton

Compare this American inaction to the "Spring of Hope" vision that is becoming a reality as the New Silk Road is bringing large-scale infrastructure across Asia, Africa, and Ibero-America—infrastructure which was denied them throughout the colonial and post-colonial eras. In particular, two of the Great Projects proposed by Lyndon LaRouche over the past decades—the Kra Canal in southern Thailand, and the Transaqua project for the replenishing of the nearly-depleted Lake Chad in Africa through diversion of water from the Congo—are now close to being launched. In both of these Great Projects, the role of China's "Belt and Road Initiative" is the central driving force, viewing mankind not as subjects of an oligarchy, but as the reason for the existence of governments.

Why can't the United States and Europe participate in this world-changing development process? The only reason is the continuing power of the bankrupt financial empire centered in London and New York—the degeneration of the Western banking system into a sprawling gambling-casino, only willing to "invest" in speculative binges, driving an ever-greater decay of the physical economy and the standard of living of the "lower 90%" of the population. This is the dreadful re-

ality which brought about the election of Donald Trump. This is also the reality which is driving the on-going coup attempt against President Trump by the powers of London and Wall Street and their slavish, totally-owned political leaders and media whores. The same financial and media elites now pushing for Trump's ouster—these are the same people who demand, "The United States must not be allowed to join the New Silk Road; the government must not interfere in Wall Street." And these are the same moneyed interests who are conspiring for U.S. war preparations against Russia.

Houston must serve as a wake-up call. Many Americans will act—but even the courage being shown daily in the rescue of stranded neighbors is not enough. We must also, finally, act to restore the Public Credit System of Alexander Hamilton—and the only way to do that is through the implementation of the policies enunciated in Lyndon LaRouche's Four Laws. The necessary steps, as elaborated by LaRouche, must be taken. The only way to prevent more Houstons is to generate the credit needed to rebuild our cities at a modern level: our transportation networks, water systems, power generation, and schools and hospitals. As Helga Zepp-LaRouche said at the Aug. 26 Manhattan forum on the infrastructure crisis, "Why not build 50 new cities?" China has done it, and is taking it around the world through the Belt and Road. We can, and must, join them.

EIR Contents

www.larouchepub.com Volume 44, Number 35, September 1, 2017

Army National Guard photo

Cover This Week

Texas National Guardsmen help residents in areas heavily flooded from the storms of Hurricane Harvey.

Helga Zepp-LaRouche: Bring the United States into the New Paradigm!

The following is an edited version of a dialogue with Helga Zepp-LaRouche that took place at a special La-Rouche PAC Manhattan Meeting on August 26, 2017. That conference, which included presentations by Mrs. LaRouche as well as a panel of experts, dealt with the necessity for the immediate implementation of Lyndon LaRouche's Four Laws. A full video of the event may be found at https://larouchepac.com/20170827/manhattan-town-hall-revive-hamilton-s-american-system-and-presidency-through-larouche-s

Helga Zepp-LaRouche: Ladies and gentlemen in New York, I'm very happy to be able to address you, because this gives me the opportunity to emphasize from my own perspective why I think that this is *the most dramatic moment in history*—in our lifetimes. If this goes in the right direction, then we could be in a completely New Paradigm, in a new set of relations among nations in a very short period of time. And if it goes in the wrong way, we would be quickly back on the course of confrontation with Russia and China, as we were with the previous administration. Given all the crisis spots and drama points of the situation, this could lead to World War III and the extinction of civilization.

I think between these two possibilities, the tension could not be greater, and obviously the place where this is fought out is the United States. Now, there is a coup in process, and I think we better go back to the article which appeared in the British magazine the *Spectator* on the 21st of January, where they—under the headline "Assassination, Coup, or Impeachment?"—discussed the need to get rid of President Trump, this only one day after his inauguration. It was quite amazing that from minute one, the trans-Atlantic establishment reacted to the election of the President with shock, with unacceptance, and with a complete demonstration of disrespect which I have never seen manifest against an American President. Now remember, that the people who put

Combat Camera

DoD photo/Staff Sgt. Kaily Brown, U.S. Army

Bush-Obama era perpetual war: Helicopter deployment in Iraq (left) and patrol in opium poppy field in Afghanistan (right).

themselves in the moral high seat, so to speak—these are the same elites who have no problem with the wars declared by Bush and Obama, wars which were based on lies, which have cost literally millions of lives in the Middle East and elsewhere. They had no problem with the drone killing; they had no problem with the civilian casualties of these drones, calling them "collateral damage." They turned a blind eye to the suffering of the people in the United States, whom Hillary Clinton called so despicably "the deplorables." They had no sympathy for the lack of development in the Middle East or in Africa, which has resulted in millions of people fleeing from these areas.

Neo-Nazi protestors in the Maidan, January 2014.

Now these liberals, who are now attacking Trump in such an arrogant way, are the self-proclaimed defenders of human rights, of democracy, of western values, and they have declared war on the Presidency of President Trump. What is the crime of President Trump in their eyes? He promised to improve the relationship with Russia; he subsequently established a very good relationship with President Xi Jinping of China. He pledged—and is in part implementing it—to end the interventionist wars; he promised to return to the American system of economy, of Alexander Hamilton, Henry C. Carey and Lincoln, and to create jobs in that tradition. And he promised to fight the horrible drug epidemic going on in the United States right now. All of these policies, however, were a threat and are a threat to the idea of a unipolar world which the neo-cons had tried to establish in collusion with the British after the collapse of the Soviet Union. It was their policies which promoted color revolution, regime change, interventionist wars—and this is on the record. Victoria Nuland, obviously in collusion with her boss, Hillary Clinton, admitted that the State Department of the Obama administration spent $5 billion in the Ukraine alone to cause regime change. Remember, the narrative about the Ukraine—namely that Putin supposedly changed the borders by force—is a complete lie, because it was the regime change policy to which Russia reacted. It was that narrative which has been one of the key reasons for the demonization of President Putin in Russia.

Due to the heroic forensic investigation of the VIPS (Veteran Intelligence Professionals for Sanity), which proved that there was no Russian hacking, but there was a leak from the inside, Russia-gate is sort of on the back burner right now, and it may go nowhere—in large part because the Schiller Institute distributed the findings of the VIPS internationally.

So now you are looking at the next phase of the coup, which started or escalated in Charlottesville, a city which was called the center of resistance against Trump by its mayor, Signer, from day one. So what happened was, you had a violent demonstration, the KKK and the white supremacists on the one side, and the Antifa on the other side—in a typical gang-countergang fashion, which was obviously permitted by the mayor and a police force that did not even keep these two groupings apart; they clashed. For everybody who remembers the role of the FBI in the Civil Rights movement, it was clearly a moment of *déjà vu*, of remembering how these gang-countergang violent escalations are controlled.

Obviously it is not Charlottesville, it is not the gangs and countergangs on the ground—but behind that is Wall Street, the neo-con operators who are orchestrating what has been called correctly a "Maidan II," in reference to the coup against the elected government of Kiev. Obviously, a third force is moving, controlling both sides. This situation has created such chaos that, for example, the official paper of the Chinese government, the *Global Times,* compared what is going on in the United States right now to the Cultural Revolution of China which lasted from 1966 to 74. That was a period which the present Chinese people and government look back on as probably the darkest moment in the history of China. Under the rule of the Gang of Four and the Red Guards, you had a reign of terror. People were taken out of their beds in the night; any intellectual was attacked. People were really living in horror. We are in danger of that climate developing in the United States. I was absolutely reminded of the last days of the Weimar republic, when the Nazis and the communists were similarly fighting it out in the streets. That is what led to the rise of Adolf Hitler. It is obvious that this whole scenario is threatening to tear the United States apart.

Xinhua

An Ethiopian driver gets on the train in Addis Ababa, Ethiopia. The Chinese-financed and -built railroad was inaugurated Oct 1, 2016.

Financial Breakdown and Remedy

Let me add one more dimension to this picture. The same financial system that the neo-cons are trying to preserve is about to collapse. The deregulation of the trans-Atlantic financial sector after the repeal—first of Bretton Woods in 1971, and then Glass-Steagall in 1999—led to these incredible excesses in speculation and then to the financial crash of 2007-2008. Ten years later, the situation is much worse than it was then. All the so-called instruments of the central banks have been used up—quantitative easing, pumping of money, negative interest rates; all of these policies have increased the state debt, the corporate debt, the student debt, the auto debt, and all of these crises could erupt at any moment, triggered by any one incident: a collapse of a large number of corporate firms, the Italian banking crisis, or any other derivative failure. Everyday, $5 trillion of currency is floating around the globe; $5 trillion every day.

There are many crises. For example, the level three derivatives; these are the derivatives which cannot be sold because they are toxic. They are sitting there like a complete bomb in the system. *Spiegel* magazine had an article warning of the next crash a couple of days ago. The former Italian economic minister Tremonti said the next crash is absolutely about to happen. So, the extreme danger is very clear. If this were to happen in an uncontrolled way, what would such a financial crash do to the already extremely explosive situation in the United States? Under those circumstances, a civil war and a plunge into complete chaos is absolutely thinkable.

There is a remedy available, and the solution is already in place. About four years ago, China's President Xi Jinping initiated, very much in cohesion with our own efforts of the Schiller Institute, a policy he called the New Silk Road. This has become, in four years, the largest infrastructure program in history. It is already—some people say, twelve times, others say twenty times, as big as the Marshall Plan. There are an unbelievable number of projects in progress: six large economic corridors in different parts of Eurasia, seventy countries cooperating fully with China, and at the Belt and Road Forum in May there were 110 countries represented. Silk Road cooperation has gained enormous traction in Latin America, but also in Europe, despite the relative opposition of the European Union. The 16+1, that is, the Central and Eastern European countries, are fully cooperating, and so are Italy, Portugal, and even France.

But the largest change in the strategic situation, as the result of the New Silk Road, has arrived in Africa, where China has built many, many projects: a railroad from Djibouti to Addis Ababa, another from Rwanda to Kenya is in progress, and many industrial parks and hydropower projects. The largest single infrastructure project in history has now been agreed upon by the Chinese government and the Italian government: the development of the Trans-Aqua project, which is the idea of bringing water from the tributaries of the Congo River to Lake Chad. This will provide irrigation to twelve countries; it will allow inland shipping; and it will change the whole agricultural situation. It is being promoted by the same

The livelihood of millions depends on Lake Chad, now severely depleted, shown in an aerial photo. The largest single infrastructure project in history, the Trans-Aqua project, bringing water from the tributaries of the Congo River to restore the lake, has now been agreed upon by the Chinese and Italian governments.

Chinese firm which built the Three Gorges Dam.

This is very, very important, because the biggest Achilles Heel, in my view, of President Trump, is the fact that all these maneuvers against him have made it virtually impossible for him to deliver on his promise to create jobs and build infrastructure worth $1 trillion. Now some jobs have obviously been created, but it has not led to the total change which FDR was able to implement with Glass-Steagall and the New Deal, and that kind of *big* change is absolutely necessary. That is what we are trying to put on the table, and maybe the crisis in New York can be the trigger point to cause that change to happen.

An End to Geopolitics

Now infrastructure normally has a life expectancy, depending on the category, of anywhere between twenty and fifty years, but most of the infrastructure of New York is already about 100 years old. As a result, you have trains derailing, you have fires in the subways, and absolute chaos. Now, compare that to China. China had built, by the end of last year, more than 20,000 km of high-speed rail systems. You can only see such high-speed rail systems in China, not in the United States or Europe. By the year 2020, China wants to have all major cities connected by high-speed rail systems. They now have a fantastic project, which I think is of the highest interest for New York. It's the idea of taking the entire region of Beijing, Tianjin, and Hebei Province, which has about 130 million people, and completely modernizing it by building a new city outside of that, to relieve the pressure on infrastructure in Beijing and around it. Now such an approach could be taken for New York, for example, because I don't think you will solve the problem of New York infrastructure by just repairing this little piece and that little piece. You need a complete grand design. China has offered to invest $1.4 trillion of its U.S. Treasuries in American infrastructure. Just a few weeks ago there was a meeting in New York, where the Chinese ambassador to Washington, Ambassador Cui, reminded people that looking back in history, there were sixteen examples where one country was economically surpassing the leading country. In twelve cases it led to war, and in four cases, the emerging country just took over the role of the old leading country. Ambassador Cui said that China does not want either of those, but wants to propose a completely new paradigm of win-win cooperation, what President Xi Jinping always calls a *community for the shared future of mankind.*

Now, many people are reluctant to accept these Chinese offers, and they think what China is doing is just pursuing its own interest, or just trying to replace Anglo-American imperialism with Chinese imperialism, e.g., to take over the raw materials of the world. But I think this is a wrong conception, because we can not stay in the geometry of geopolitics, of the idea that you have a legitimate interest of one country or a group of countries against another group of countries—or even worse, of maintaining a unipolar position, where you will not allow any other country to become stronger. Well, China has 1.4 billion, and India has more than 1.3 billion people. The idea that the United States will be the unipolar power forever is just not realistic. We have to find a different approach.

The problem is that many think-tanks, and especially the mainstream media, look at this like looking into a mirror. What they see in the mirror is their own face, namely evil intentions, geopolitical games, imperialist domination, manipulating the rules to your own benefit, and promoting color revolutions. So they have these policies, and they just project the mirror of their own evil thinking. It is quite interesting, that the German magazine *Der Spiegel*, which is the German word for "mirror," has exactly that name.

What China is proposing is a completely new paradigm—win-win cooperation, which is based on very clear principles of non-interference into the internal affairs of other countries, respect for the sovereignty, and the interest, of the other. People have to grapple with that concept. What we are talking about is a completely new paradigm, a completely new idea that you have to put the interest of mankind first, and then comes the interest of any individual country. Now that method was developed for the first time by Nicholas of Cusa, a great thinker of the 15th Century, who developed a method of thinking of the coincidence of opposites—the idea that the human creative reason is able to formulate a level where the one is of a higher magnitude, of a higher order, than the many, and that you can, on the basis of reason, find that higher level of interest, where the conflicts of the many are solved on a higher plateau.

Now, this method of thinking is not just a philosophical conception. It was the basis for the Peace of Westphalia, and it is presently the effort to replace military solutions with diplomatic solutions. Fortunately, this is already happening in various parts of the world, despite back-and-forth and disturbances. One very good example of where this method is working is Syria, where because of President Trump's collaboration with Putin, there is a ceasefire in almost all of Syria right now. You have right now—in the last couple of days—a very large industrial fair in Damascus, with high-level delegations from China, from India, and from Japan—and the reconstruction of Syria is now on the table. Six hundred thousand Syrian refugees have already moved back, and there is hope that many more can return to their homes. In Afghanistan, despite the very unfortunate announcement of President Trump that he will send more troops to Afghanistan, there are other initiatives. For example, the Afghan government has just invited India, Pakistan, Iran, Russia, the United States, and China to participate in the reconstruction of Af-

Calm is being maintained and displaced persons are beginning to return to Southwest Syria, as the U.S. and Russia collaborate in ceasefire.

ghanistan, and that must be the solution.

As to the Korea crisis, South Korean President Moon has reconstituted the Northern Economic Commission, and in that way signalled that he is intending to go back to the Sunshine Policy of President Kim Daejung, which is the idea of collaboration between South Korea and North Korea, together with Russia and China, in the development of North Korea.

Win-Win Policy for the World

Now the same approach must be taken in the United States. Just a few days ago, the civil rights leader Andrew Young responded to the events in Charlottesville by making exactly that point. He said the reason for these clashes is not race; the reason is poverty. Therefore, the way to solve this crisis is to create jobs. Now that is the American system of economy. This is what Henry C. Carey was talking about when he talked about a harmony of interests.

Now this is very urgent, because of the danger of the financial collapse, because of the danger of a social explosion in the United States. What must be put on the table urgently is the Glass-Steagall law of Franklin D. Roosevelt, in combination with the other laws proposed by my husband Lyndon LaRouche—which are for Glass-Steagall, a national bank, a credit system, and then a crash program for the development of fusion power and international cooperation in space technology, because you very urgently need a huge jump in the productivity of the economy.

Now the renewal of the New York infrastructure can be the key trigger to put such a change on the agenda. I think the only way it will function is to think about it as part of this global change, of all these development approaches to Syria, Afghanistan, North Korea, and many other parts of the world. If this happens, then the United States could participate in the AIIB, the Asian Infrastructure Development Bank. American corporations could participate in many of the projects of the Belt and Road Initiative, Chinese firms and engineers could invest in the United States, and you would have a completely new world in a very short period of time.

Now, global peace and social peace in the United States are part of the same new paradigm, and in both cases, *the new name for peace is development.* Thank you. [Applause]

Question: I'm Elliot Greenspan. Recently, in a piece in the *Economist* by Steve Bannon, in looking at the Chinese initiatives for global development, Bannon says, "We're going to screw the One Belt One Road," and he counterposes Judeo-Christianity to what he calls the mercantilist-Confucian order. He calls for the triumph, over the next generations, of "Judeo-Christianity" against the "mercantilist-Confucian order." You had addressed some of this at two prior conferences this year, and I think it would be invaluable for you to set the record straight: What is it exactly that China is actually proposing? What is the Confucian order and so on? And how is it that we have a potential for a coincidence of opposites, so to speak, here?

Zepp-LaRouche: I don't know what is going on in the head of Mr. Bannon, but I can assure you that most of the people who oppose the Belt and Road Initiative in Chinese policy, are doing that for quite different reasons than they say. They claim that it's democracy and Western values and all of these things, but in reality it is the geopolitical control of the world. And therefore, I think it is important that people study what China is actually doing. Read the speeches of President Xi Jinping, and you will find that he expresses a completely different philosophy, namely a harmony of world development, based on the Confucian tradition, which after all is the tradition of 2,500 years of Chinese history, only briefly interrupted by the Cultural Revolution, which deliberately turned against it.

The Confucian idea of harmony is based on the maximum development of the individual, the self-perfection, lifelong learning, and improvement of the character; and based on that idea, everyone is challenged to become a wise person and a noble person. I have made the comparison to Friedrich Schiller's idea of *Aestheti-*

cal Education, where there is also the idea that each individual must become a beautiful soul, a beautiful character. Pursuing lifelong self-perfection of your mind and your character—this is the model, then, of a harmonious development of a family. That all the members of the family should strive toward the maximum development of all the other family members. You all know that in a good family, this is how the parents care for their children, or how the children care about their grandparents. A harmonious family, even if it has become a rarity in these modern times, has been the foundation of any functioning society, not only in China but actually everywhere.

That idea is then, for Confucius, the model of the harmonious development of the whole country; and by extension, the harmonious development of all nations on this planet.

Samuel Huntington, the evil author of *The Soldier and the State* and the *Clash of Civilizations,* claimed in this ridiculous book—which only proved that he knows nothing about Christianity, or Confucius, or Islam, or Hinduism—that Asian philosophy is incapable of universal conceptions. That's not true! There is only one leader right now, who in a clear form, speaks about the one humanity, the community of a shared future, and a community of common principles, and that is Xi Jinping.

If you look at the reason the Chinese model is so attractive, it is not because it is offering military alliances, but is offering economic benefits for all countries which participate. China accomplished an unbelievable economic miracle in thirty years, lifting 800 million people out of poverty and creating a very sizable middle-level income bracket. Now their plan is to eliminate the remaining four percent of poverty by the year 2020.

China has, without any question, contributed the most to eliminating poverty, not only in China, but in many other countries, by offering the Chinese model to participating countries, countries that are part of the Belt and Road Initiative. The facts simply speak for themselves: For example, countries in Africa are optimistic for the first time that they can overcome poverty and underdevelopment, because of China—not because of the European Union, not because of the United States, but because of Chinese investments in infrastructure.

So there are, in a certain sense, facts to prove that China is, indeed, doing what they are claiming to do, and that is the reason that the Chinese model has developed a tremendous attractiveness around the world.

I would suggest to people who have doubts about what I an saying—don't simply believe me, but start with reading the speeches of Xi Jinping, and look at the tremendous success story of China. If you take a vacation, travel to China—go to these places, talk to the people, and you will see that people are optimistic.

I just wrote an article about good government and bad government, which has been an issue since the Renaissance. I think government is not a "self-purpose": Government is there, as the American Constitution says, for the happiness of the people. I think that all of these factors should help to overcome the prejudices which are spread by all the American think-tanks, and most of the German think-tanks. Unfortunately, Mr. Bannon seems to be very uninformed about what is going on, and maybe it's a good thing he's no longer there in the Trump Administration to spread his ideas.

Uplift the People

Question: This is Alvin in New York. We, in New York and throughout the country as a part of this movement, this organization—it's been made clear to us how it is now our responsibility to awaken and uplift the citizens who are otherwise terribly demoralized and confused.

Yesterday, I viewed once again, an address that Mr. LaRouche gave in 2004 in Talladega, Alabama, where on the occasion of talking about Dr. Martin Luther King, LaRouche noted the qualities of leadership Dr. King possessed, and the association, in Lyn's mind, of having the Crucifixion of Christ embedded within him. LaRouche went on to describe the case of Joan of Arc, her story, and thirdly the tragedy of Hamlet, which all seem very relevant to us now.

So I was wondering, since it is our job: can you talk to us more about that kind of love and agape—that type of leadership which is the only thing that can move people; that we have to demonstrate to them now?

Zepp-LaRouche: Well, it is very clear that people are struggling with demoralization. This is not only the case for the United States, but since we organize in Europe as well, we have noticed, even though the dynamic is quite different—because you have the Trump voters in the United States, of whom you have very few in Europe—but people are now worried. When Trump started to do the first things, like the meeting in Mar-a-Lago, the sending of Mr. Pottinger to the Belt and Road Forum, the ceasefire in Syria, people were actually very optimistic that Trump, indeed, was going in a completely different direction.

But then all of these attacks occurred. "Russiagate" was pounded in every day, new attacks from former intelligence heads from the Obama period, and the media campaign—the media in principle is *only* reporting negatively. Just to give you an idea, the *Washington Post* and the *New York Times,* which are the worst enemies in the campaign against Trump, have about 84% negative coverage; but the First German Television Channel has 98% negative views! So you can imagine that if people only watch these mainstream media, which are absolutely controlled by this neo-con apparatus, that people become depressed and demoralized.

Indeed, I would be telling you something wrong, if I said you can sit calmly and watch this thing, because it *is* extremely dangerous. Just think about all the open assassination threats coming against Trump: The *Julius Caesar* performance in New York, all the so-called Hollywood celebrities openly threatening, saying they could imagine assassination, ripping down the White House, and the unbelievable use of language. And then naturally this orchestration which you saw in Charlottesville, which was really an extremely evil thing. So there *is* reason to be extremely concerned.

But I think you have to look at the dangers without getting paralyzed, and without giving up, because the potential obviously is still there. And what I said earlier about the cease-fire in Syria, the hopeful signs, despite all the negative problems in Afghanistan, South Korea—these are indeed absolutely the beginnings of settling conflicts, all of which could have been the trigger for World War III.

I think it requires exactly this quality which you mentioned, which Lyndon LaRouche spoke about so beautifully in the Talladega speech: that when you are confronted with a great danger—but you know that the outcome of history for many generations to come depends on your own courage and your own activity— then you have to rise above your own life, and you have to call forth within yourself this quality of the Sublime, which Schiller spoke about so beautifully. Schiller said, if man is merely a mortal being, the threat to his physical existence will cause him to have fear. But what if you connect your life to ideas and principles which are bigger than your own life—like what will happen to the United States for generations to come? How can we intersect this historic conjuncture so that we overcome, for the very first time in history, the idea that you solve conflict with war? An idea which we should absolutely give up, because if you use thermonuclear weapons, that is the end, and civilization may just cease to exist.

We are at a point in history where people have to really become heroic, and fearless, and optimistic, and happy. Once you have all of these qualities mobilized in yourself, I think we can absolutely make a miracle, because I believe that there is something in the laws of the universe which gives us a chance to win. It is that quality about which Leibniz spoke, saying that a great force of evil catalyzes an even greater force of good, because that is the true freedom of the human being. I think the universe is made that way, and there are laws in this universe which you can call "natural law"; in other parts of the planet they call it cosmic laws. But there *is* a lawfulness in the universe which, if you do what you have to do—some people call it providence, some people call it just performing your historical responsibility—I think if we fulfill this, I think as Schiller said, even the longest arm of the tyrant can be pulled down, and we will win this battle—so be courageous! [applause]

Question: In order to become more courageous, sometimes people have to free themselves from the grip of deep lies. While we've been making tremendous progress in getting Americans to see China differently—it's very different than even six months ago—yet there's no question that there's anger over what happened in the 1970s, with so many American jobs being shipped to China. I would like to ask you to comment on my own personal view of this, which is that when Nixon and Kissinger went to China, that while they went there to win China over against Russia, they also pursued the idea of China becoming the chief labor outpost of the United States, and that China was desperate for some kind of transformation. You're an authority on this. Actually, *China Daily* just published a beautiful article in which you talk about your own visit there in 1971, and I've always wanted you to say something about this, about how they got drawn into that agenda.

NASA

Deng Xiaoping (center) and his wife Zhuo Lin (right of him) being briefed by Johnson Space Center director Christopher C. Kraft (right front) on Feb. 2, 1979.

Zepp-LaRouche: It is really funny because when I was in China in the summer of 1971, that was the moment when it was announced that Kissinger would come. I was surprised. Everybody else was surprised because this was the middle of the Cultural Revolution, and the talk about the United States at that time was that U.S. imperialism is just a paper tiger, meaning that it's not very strong. You had a completely different dynamic then. China of the Cultural Revolution is the opposite of what China is now. Because of the reforms of Deng Xiaoping, they have completely rejected everything that was associated with the Gang of Four. You have to imagine, they are as different as the Germany of the Classical period and the Germany of National Socialism. I mean you wouldn't blame Schiller (unless you're an idiot of the Frankfurt School) for what happened in the twelve years of the Nazi regime, and you wouldn't compare present-day Germany with those twelve years. You wouldn't compare the previous sixteen years of U.S. policy of Obama and Bush with the American Revolution. In the history of a country, you have completely different periods, depending on which faction takes over. When Kissinger and Nixon started the opening-up, it had exactly this geopolitical dimension against Russia, and in the first years of the opening up, China was completely a cheap labor market for the United States and for Europe.

We opposed that. I remember that we criticized this tremendously. We said this is not in the interest of China. It's not in the interest of the United States. In the United States, it destroys jobs, and in China the cheap labor income does not pay for the cost of living for the population. It was a form of looting. While China was able to accumulate a certain amount of foreign currency and wealth doing that, it did so at the expense of the environment. China has very significant environmental problems—air pollution, polluted water—and this was because the cheap-labor production was just that, cheap labor. It didn't protect the environment; it did not protect the labor force. I visited some factories at that time, and people were putting together transistor radios and things like that under sweatshop conditions. It was just completely horrible. It was really a bad policy, and it was completely rejected by Deng Xiaoping after the death of Mao, when the Gang of Four could be kicked out.

Deng Xiaoping had sent economic delegations to the United States and to European countries, and they studied there. In France, in Germany, and in Holland, they studied Friedrich List, and step-by-step, they replaced this cheap-labor production with the present policy which is completely the opposite. China, by applying this Confucian, Listian, Carey method of economy, has now put all their emphasis on excellence, on leap-frogging to the most modern technologies. As a result, China is now the avant-garde and the leader in many areas, like for example, high-speed train systems. They're building the best high-speed train systems in the world right now. They have 20,000 kilometers (probably more by now) of high-speed rail while the United States has exactly 250 miles of high-speed rail, which goes 250 km/h at high speed, which is nothing. China already has trains that go 320 km/h and soon they will have trains that go 400 km/h.

www.ibnlive.com

By 2012, China's space program sent its first female astronaut Liu Yang into space when it launched Shenzhou 9 to dock with its prototype space lab.

In other areas like fusion research, nuclear power, space research, China is now absolutely leap-frogging to number one; and in a certain sense, that worry of the trade union leaders and others in the United States that China is stealing jobs is not true. I mean just think what enormous potential will open up if the United States would cooperate with the Belt and Road Initiative. It could rebuild its own middle-level industry. They could invest in all of the projects in Latin America, Africa, and along the Eurasian Land-Bridge. It would completely change the situation, and also rebuild the United States. You could have complete change in the United States. You could have fifty new cities. Why not build fifty new cities? Between the coasts, there are many states which are extremely thinly populated, with almost no cities—you could connect those cities with those of the coasts with the high-speed rail system, and you could have science cities. People have to have a power of imagination. China has done these things and is doing these things, also in other countries—China-Ecuador, China to places in Africa.

I think it is really important to imagine a completely different system. If the United States would now do what Franklin D. Roosevelt did—a New Deal, Glass-Steagall, and cooperate with China—the United States could experience an industrial revolution bigger than at any time in its own history. People have to understand that we are right now at the end of a system, a system which cannot be saved. We need to replace it with a completely new system. People just have a hard time imagining that, but there are examples of such changes. For example, the Marshall Plan in Europe was such an example, and the Meiji Restoration in Japan was such an example—so was what Roosevelt did with the New Deal. People have to grasp that such a dramatic change is absolutely possible today.

Question: This is Daniel in New York. I want to encourage everyone here to come out in the street with us and in every capacity, both at our public tables and interventions at town hall meetings, at conferences, and all the types of things that we need to do. Now's the time to act with us. I want to report that particularly in the recent period, there's been an explosive response to the effort to defeat this coup. We have been going to areas around New York City, and we also have people all across the country, including on the West Coast and in Michigan, who are finding people running up to our tables to join the LaRouche Movement in defending Trump and in creating this economic breakthrough for our nation.

I recently read with a couple of people a paper by Lyndon LaRouche which he dictated from prison, after he was railroaded into prison by Robert Mueller and others, which is *In the Garden of Gethsemane*, in which he says that only those revolutions that appeal to the divine spark of reason within the individual will succeed. It seemed to me that this represented a different concept of intelligence from what we commonly understand in the culture today. I wanted to ask you if you have any comment on that, with this in mind of getting much more mobilization in public activity from our supporters and friends.

Zepp-LaRouche: The enemy, as you say, does not really have a lot of methods. All they can say is that the Belt and Road Initiative will collapse because so much credit is financed by Chinese banks—but the difference is very simple. If you look at the enormous amounts of real production, infrastructure, factories, industrial parks, railways, hydropower projects, and bridges—the credit invested in the Belt and Road Initiative has resulted in real wealth. If you look at Wall Street and the City of London, on the contrary; they are investing in paper—not even paper but electronic figures in a computer. They say the Belt and Road Initiative will collapse because of this credit policy, but the reality is that the Belt and Road Initiative is already everywhere. Just because you don't read it in the media, doesn't mean it doesn't exist.

I was talking to some people in Europe in the last couple of days in different countries, and they all said, "Your policy is winning. It's coming. You know you were one important influence. This is your policy." So, people who've known us for a long time know that, and therefore, you should just make sure that many people know about this alternative, because once people know that there is a completely different system, people start to think completely differently, and they become angry that they are being told lies, or the truth is being withheld from them. I think right now the key thing is to be confident that once people know this, then they change. I think we have a tremendous moment. All it requires is for President Trump to announce something big, like Roosevelt did with the New Deal. I don't put it beyond President Trump that he can do that. I think President Trump has the character, he has the temperament to surprise his opponents, and I think that we should create an environment in the country to encourage him to do that. We have to increase the pressure from the population for Trump to go for a grand design for the United States, to be bigger than the pressure by Wall Street for him to remain within the box. They want to box him in. They threaten that if he doesn't capitulate, they'll kill him or impeach him. The way to get President Trump out of the box is by having a lot of people demand that he keep his promise of $1 trillion or preferably $8 trillion investment in infrastructure. I think that you have to have an absolute optimism that this can be done. It's not Congress. The international environment for it already exists, so all we need to do is to get the American population to demand that Trump do what he proposed, and everything can be solved quickly.

With this mobilization, I think we should aim to find people in the Democratic Party who are not completely crazy (and I'm convinced that there must be some) and those people in the trade unions and other institutions, and basically use this absolutely unique opportunity. As long as President Trump is in office, that change can be effected. I think if we appeal to this option then people will have the courage, and I think it is the heart, and it's the passion for humanity, which will make the difference, and not the algorithms of Wall Street. [applause]

Identifying with China

by Chen Weihua, originally published by *China Daily USA*

Helga Zepp-LaRouche sees Belt and Road Initiative as fulfilling lifelong pursuit by her and her US political activist husband, Lyndon LaRouche.

Aug. 18—Helga Zepp-LaRouche was 23 in 1971 when she embarked on a Swedish cargo ship to travel the world. The trip took her to a number of African and Asian countries and included several months in China.

The young German had just finished her training as a journalist. "My generation was still curious about the world. The youth of today, they just Google about things from the search machine. I want to see what the world looks like," she told *China Daily*.

China was still in the midst of the "cultural revolution" (1966-1976), and as the ship had to be repaired in Shanghai, Helga had time to observe Chinese society and interact with local people.

She saw gray-painted warships at the mouth of the Yangtze River. She attended organized tours, visited people's homes, factories and a children's palace, and she heard modern Peking Opera played on loudspeakers.

She also met German-speaking Chinese, discussing with them politics and learning what life was like in China at that time. She found people were "kind" but said, "People were not happy at all."

Helga also traveled to Qingdao, a seaside city in

Top: Helga Zepp-LaRouche speaks to China Daily in an interview. Chen Weihua / China Daily; Left: Helga Zepp-LaRouche poses for a photo during her attendance at the Belt and Road Forum for International Cooperation in Beijing in May. Provided to China Daily; Right: Helga Zepp-LaRouche in 1971 photo taken during her first trip to China. Provided to China Daily

Shandong province that had a lot of German influence, as well as to Tianjin and Beijing.

In Beijing, she toured places like the Summer Palace and was even tempted to learn Chinese but soon realized that it would be difficult and take a long time. "You have to stay here, or you forget it. But anyway, it really started my interest in China," she said.

Helga, who now travels frequently in China, felt it was fortunate for her to see China at a time of "cultural revolution" (1966-76).

Life-changing trip

Of her seafaring in 1971, Helga said she was shocked by the extreme poverty she saw in Africa. She described it as "such a shocking experience" and seeing Africa "from the bottom."

"I came back from this trip with the absolute conviction that the world had to change, had to be improved," she said.

Back in Germany, Helga tried to look for a theory to fix the problem that haunted her. She found Lyndon LaRouche, a U.S. political activist better known for launching the LaRouche Movement.

The movement, which has included many organizations and companies in the world, promotes a revival of classical art and greater commitment to science; advocates the development of major economic infrastructure projects on a global scale; and calls for reform of the world financial system to encourage investment in the physical economy and suppress financial speculation.

Helga found Lyndon to be the only one who talked about the need for the development and industrialization of Africa and Third World countries, as well as the establishment of an international development bank, something like the Asian Infrastructure Investment Bank (AIIB) today.

"Then I became part of the movement," she said. On Dec 29, 1977, the two got married in Wiesbaden, a city in west central Germany.

Helga said she did not follow the Third World theory of then-Chinese leader Chairman Mao Zedong but paid more attention to the Non-Aligned Movement headquartered in Indonesia.

She has met some world leaders such as Indian Prime Minister Indira Gandhi and Mexican President Jose Lopez-Portillo.

Helga said they had been promoting the idea of development of a Eurasian land bridge through infrastructure in the early 1990s, but did not receive a positive response from the U.S. "The only government which responded positively was China," she said.

In 1996, she returned to China for the first time to attend and speak at a meeting on Eurasian development. She found a China totally different from the one of 25 years before. The hundreds of thousands of bicycles on the streets had been replaced by cars.

But she said that comparing 1996 to today, China's development has been more phenomenal. "The Chinese economic model is really the most successful model," she said, adding that China has lifted hundreds of millions of people out of poverty in recent decades.

Since then, she has frequently traveled there, often speaking at think tanks, including the China Institute of Contemporary International Relations (CICIR) and the Chinese Academy of Social Sciences (CASS).

During a trip in 2014 to explore the ancient Silk Road in Northwest China's Gansu province, Helga was amazed to see the construction of the Lanzhou-Urumqi railroad going at full steam simultaneously in various spots, literally in the desert. The 1,776-kilometer (1,100 miles) line went into operation at the end of that year.

Belt and Road Initiative

Helga was excited when President Xi Jinping unveiled the Belt and Road Initiative (BRI) in 2013. The BRI, which was then known as the Silk Road Economic Belt and the 21st Century Maritime Silk Road, is a development strategy proposed by Xi to focus on connectivity and cooperation between countries.

She hasn't stopped talking about it since. The Schiller Institute she founded in 1984 also has published significantly on the subject.

In May, Helga went to Beijing to participate in the Belt and Road Forum for International Cooperation, a meeting that drew 29 heads of state and representatives from more than 100 countries.

"I was really happy to be able to participate because we've been fighting for this for so long. I sort of identify with the success of this project," she said.

Helga had chatted with many people from Africa to Latin America attending the meeting and found that they shared the same experience. "We were proud to be part of the historical moment of the birth of a new paradigm of mankind. It was a very strong feeling," she said.

She said she was extremely impressed by Xi's

speech, calling it "very rich" and reflecting the ideas of a Confucian philosopher and harmony.

The Schiller Institute also has sponsored conferences in cities across the U.S., from San Francisco to Detroit and New York, promoting the BRI and urging the US to participate.

Unlike the Obama administration, which was more resistant to the Chinese initiatives of AIIB (Asia Infrastructure Investment Bank) and BRI, U.S. President Donald Trump has put infrastructure construction atop his agenda and sent an interagency delegation, led by Matthew Pottinger, a National Security Council senior director for East Asia, to the Beijing forum.

Helga believes that China's financing could help build infrastructure in the US. She claims that the US needs to build 40,000 miles of fast train routes if it wants to match China's plan to connect every large city by fast train by the year 2020.

"The US economy would experience a tremendous boost through such a grand-scale infrastructural investment and could in turn export into the fast-growing Chinese market, and once competition is replaced by cooperation, the opportunities for joint ventures between the US and China in third countries are enormous," she said in May in a seminar in Beijing.

Helga has repeatedly expressed her admiration for Xi's call that "we have to have a community for a shared future of humanity."

She told a seminar in July that the BRI is not just about infrastructure and economic growth, but a new paradigm in which geopolitics is overcome.

Africa development

Helga also was happy to see the growing Chinese investment in Africa.

"If you look at Africa, without Chinese investment, Africa would have no hope. Now people have hope," she said, and told of two Chinese companies that built a 752-km electric railway linking Ethiopia's capital Addis Ababa and the port of Djibouti, where most of landlocked Ethiopia's trade flows.

In late May, Kenya also inaugurated its largest infrastructure project in more than 50 years—a $3.2 billion railway funded by China linking the capital Nairobi with the port of Mombasa.

Helga was especially excited that China is also help-

ing build a new railway linking Rwanda, Uganda and Congo, a train that she said will go into the heart of Africa "for the first time."

"I have talked with many African diplomats who said for the first time they see the horizon of overcoming poverty and obstacles for development through the help of China," she said.

She was disappointed that Europeans talk about human rights and democracy but not development in Africa, and it was the Chinese who have been doing the development work.

A report released in May by Ernst & Young said China has invested in 293 FDI (foreign direct investment) projects in Africa, with total investment of $66.4 billion, creating 130,750 jobs. Bilateral trade between China and Africa also exceeded $137 billion in 2016.

Besides trade and FDI, Chinese companies and state-related entities have financed and built many infrastructure projects across the continent, including ports, roads, railways, dams, telecom networks, power stations, and airports, the report said.

The report also said that the BRI could prove to be a win-win situation for China and Africa.

Helga dismissed the slight by some in the West about Chinese motivation in Africa, citing a seminar she attended in Frankfurt, Germany, when the Ethiopian consul general was asked if China had an "ulterior motive."

"No, because Ethiopia almost has no raw materials," Helga quoted the Ethiopian diplomat as saying.

Helga said what China is doing has justified what she and her colleagues have done for the last 40 years.

"We are very happy. It is one thing for a small organization like ours to produce ideas, but it's a quite different thing that the largest country in the world started to do it," she said.

Helga said she felt sorry that her husband has not yet been to China. "He would have enjoyed it so much to come. Now he is 94, so it will be difficult, but not impossible. Maybe one day he will come," she said.

"He loves China. He is convinced that the Chinese initiative (BRI) is the most important on the planet right now," she said.

chenweihua@chinadailyusa.com

Reprinted with permission from China Daily.

What John F. Kennedy Did To Turn the Economy Around

by Lyndon H. LaRouche, Jr.

This article, written in late 1991, is taken from Chapter V of the Schiller Institute's 173 page Science Policy Memo of August 1992, "Cold Fusion: Challenge to U.S. Policy." **EIR** *published an abridged version of that chapter in Volume 21, Number 1, January 1, 1994 without the footnotes included in the full Science Policy Memo. We have added back in certain footnotes that are required to understand some of LaRouche's more technical economic text. We have also added back La-Rouche's concluding section, "Satan Sells 'Junk Bonds'." The full Memo is available as an eBook through Google Play or Amazon.*

The assassination of our President John F. Kennedy defined the end of an era in U.S. public life. To locate the significance of that assassination—and new attempts against France's President de Gaulle during the same period, and the shifting of Germany's Chancellor Konrad Adenauer—we should first examine the economic follies of the preceding Truman and Eisenhower administrations.

Kennedy's administration launched a vigorous economic recovery from the ruinous doldrums persisting into 1961, in the wake of the deep, 1957-58 recession. The key features of that successful Kennedy recovery package included:

1. The Investment Tax-Credit Tax-Reform.
2. The Moon-Landing Goal.
3. The Acceleration of Infrastructure Building.

Some apologists for Eisenhower's administration have insisted that the aerospace and infrastructure programs of the 1960s were already partially under way during the post-Sputnik years of the 1950s. It would be misleading to argue, as those apologists have done, that Kennedy "merely accelerated" Eisenhower programs. In this case, *greater* or *lesser* represented directly opposing economic policies.

During the mid-1950s, Eisenhower had virtually mothballed a Huntsville rocket program which could have put a satellite into orbit by about 1955. Even when Khrushchov had succeeded in putting up the Sputnik, Eisenhower did not unleash the U.S. Army's Huntsville, ready and waiting capabilities; only after the humiliating failure of the competing U.S. services' "Flopnik" programs, was Redstone allowed to unfurl its capability. Thus, under Eisenhower, there would not have been a viable U.S. aerospace program at the beginning of the 1960s, if Moscow's Sputnik had not shamed the Republican administration into tolerating a post-1957 spectrum of aerospace-oriented science education and cohering projects and programs.

It is necessary, to put the details into a proper historical context, to note the points of similarity among the recovery measures of President Kennedy, and the philosophy of practice of such European leaders as President Charles de Gaulle of France, Chancellor Konrad Adenauer of pre-1964 Germany, or Italy's nation-building Enrico Mattei. We may, with apologies to Apollo priest Plutarch, see a parallel in, on the one side, Kennedy's succession to the Eisenhower 1950s, and de Gaulle's superseding of the rotting, decadent French Fourth Republic. Looking beyond 1963, we compare Kennedy's economic successes with President Johnson's disastrous aping of Prime Minister Harold Wilson's Britain, and so on. Such comparisons—fore and aft—are required, to put sharply into focus the terrible, downhill trends in U.S. economic policy of practice since the assassination of President Kennedy, nearly twenty-eight years ago.

Ask, what did Kennedy do, in the early 1960s, which Truman should have begun during the late 1940s, or Eisenhower during the 1950s? We shall soon come to that. Then, we shall see what puts the Kennedy years into a specific historic focus, and shows more clearly the pathological character of U.S. economic policy-shaping since 1963.

The follies of the Eisenhower administration's economic policies are epitomized by the influence of the President's key economic adviser, Federal Reserve Chairman Arthur Burns. On these accounts, the differences between Truman and Eisenhower were minimal.

What the U.S.A. should have done, coming out of World War II, was to have shifted a large ration of freed-up industrial capacity and labor force into a combination of accelerated infrastructure building, and a great enlargement of the advanced machine-tool sector's output, rather than the lunatic kinds of austerity measures deployed. In the take-down from peak levels of Korean War mobilization, the Eisenhower administration made what were, relative to altered circumstances, the same principled kind of errors as Truman earlier. On this account, if one considers the significant changes in secondary features of general economic circumstances which had occurred over the 1946-52 interval, the philosophical differences in economic policy thinking between the Truman and Eisenhower administrations were mere rhetoric, politically cosmetic.

The similar flaws of economic policy in those two preceding postwar administrations place the historical character of the Kennedy administration's achievements in clear focus. There were fundamental differences in U.S. policy-making after Kennedy's assassination; but, there were some significant points on which Johnson and Nixon resumed the blundering errors of

Speaking before a joint session of Congress on May 25, 1961, President John F. Kennedy committed the United States "to land a man on the Moon and return him safely to Earth." Kennedy's bold policy reforms in economy were an escape from the intellectual morass of the Eisenhower 1950s.

Truman and Eisenhower. Acknowledging those points of similarity puts the fundamental differences into clearer focus. To appreciate the significance of this point one must consider the following addenda to the earlier chapters' identifications of principles of economic science:

1. We have already stressed, repeatedly, that the primary source of both the increase, and even mere maintenance of potential population-density, is the realization of scientific progress as increases in the per-capita and per-hectare productive powers of labor by means of both increases in the per-capita standard of nuclear-family household "marketbasket," and technological progress in both the design of goods and the relevant productive processes.

2. The link between scientific progress and technological progress in product and mode of production, is the relationship between the experimental apparatus of a valid crucial experiment, and the corresponding new technological principle of design employed by tool builders.

3. These technological advances require a twofold

increase, in quality as well as quantity, in power-supplies employed. Quantity must increase geometrically; "energy-flux density" of applied power must be increased.

4. These technological advances require increases in water supplies per-capita and per-hectare.

5. These advances increase the per-capita and per-hectare quantities of both *ton-mile hours* and *ton-mile-hour-dollar*[1] of required density of freight transport per-capita and per-hectare.

6. These advances cannot be realized adequately without coordinate increases in (a) fundamental scientific progress, in (b) buildup of the technologically advancing machine-tool sector, and (c) fostering of capital-intensive, energy-intensive modes of investment in the new technologies which fundamental scientific progress is developing "upstream" from the production line.

The design of a sound monetary, tax, and financial policy must be subordinated, "enslaved" to the mission implicit in these connections. Here, on this point, lies the United States' single, original, and most important contribution to the science and practice of political economy, a principle of which virtually all U.S. university graduates today are pathologically ignorant, a principle which Truman and Eisenhower violated savagely, with rather disastrous ultimate results.

How National Banking Works

Our present U.S. Federal Reserve System is, among its other faults, *unconstitutional*. Look it up, as the fellow said: How does Article I of the *Constitution* specify the issue of U.S. currency? "Where and when," one challenges apologists for "the Fed," "was that provision of our Constitution repealed by amendment?" Never, of course. Now, put that provision of Article I, which (later) U.S. Treasury Secretary Alexander Hamilton had a hand in drafting, with Treasury Secretary Hamilton's *Report to the Congress on the Subject of a National Bank*. View that report in conjunction with

two other key reports to Congress by that Treasury Secretary, *Report on Public Credit* and *Report on Manufactures*. There you have the germ of the "American System of Political-Economy," as later elaborated by Mathew and Henry C. Carey, and by Friedrich List.

This "American System" was installed by President George Washington, overturned—to disastrous effect—by Gallatin-duped Presidents Thomas Jefferson and James Madison. It was restored under Presidents James Monroe and John Quincy Adams. It was wrecked in 1832, causing the 1837 Panic, by bankers' agent and President Andrew Jackson. It was partially restored by the Whig Party under the leadership of Speaker of the House Henry Clay. Under Presidents Pierce and Buchanan, the nation suffered disastrously. President Lincoln's brilliantly successful economic mobilization for war was conspicuously informed by American System principles. President Andrew Johnson was a British liberal's delight, a national economic and social disaster. The destruction of U.S. sovereignty in its monetary affairs was effected through the treasonous U.S. Specie Resumption Act of the late 1870s.

The final blow to the U.S. Constitution's monetary law, came through the immoral actions of former President Theodore Roosevelt, in running a Bull Moose "spoiler" candidacy, to elect Federal Reserve advocate Woodrow Wilson as President. Since that time, "Hamiltonian" American System principles have been employed only in a distorted, partial way, as U.S. war-economy mobilizations. With the Hemingway figure of Theodore Roosevelt, the Buggers had won—apparently forever.

Nonetheless, as the two great U.S. depressions under that Federal Reserve System highlight this fact, the "Hamiltonian" American System remains the only sane choice of U.S. economic policy which the United States has experienced, or observed in use among other nations, to the present day.

Although writers including Benjamin Franklin, Alexander Hamilton, Mathew Carey, Henry C. Carey, Friedrich List, and others, have documented the principles of the American System as thoroughly as any liberal or Marxian competitor has been presented, the modern development of the American System, as a system, has been accomplished only by the author of the present proposal-report. Therefore, some additional points of special reference are now summarized here.

From moment to moment, all of the domestically

---

1. The law of physical movement of freight is measured in tons moved per one mile (or a multiple thereof) per hour. Similarly, we use passenger-miles per hour. The countervailing consideration, is the social cost of delay in arrival of freight at its destined place of purchase for use. The greater the social cost of production of that freight, per ton, the greater the imputable social cost of delay. As a crude but broadly useful rule of thumb, we measure estimated social cost as dollars of assessed valuation per ton.

Census

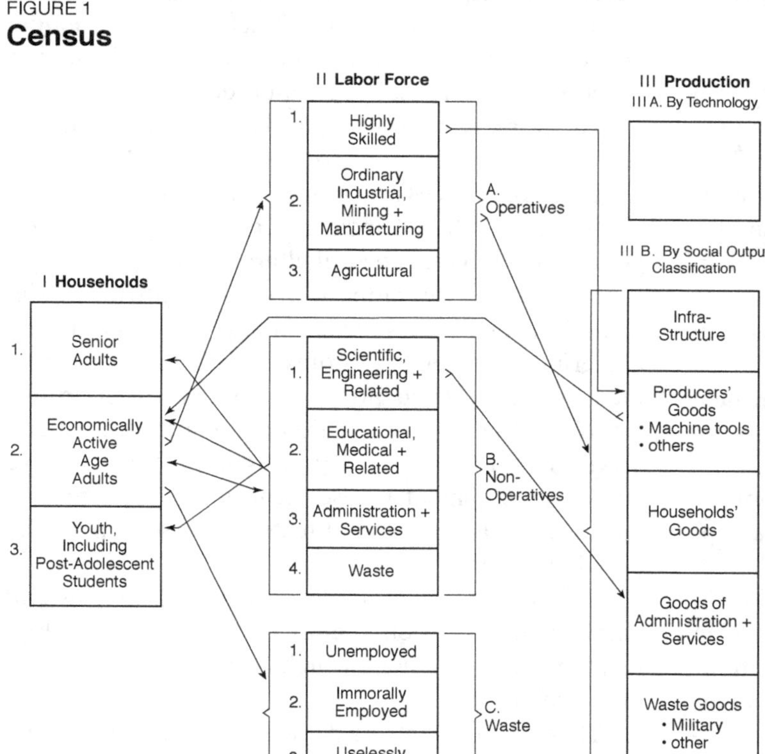

Flow Diagram of Census

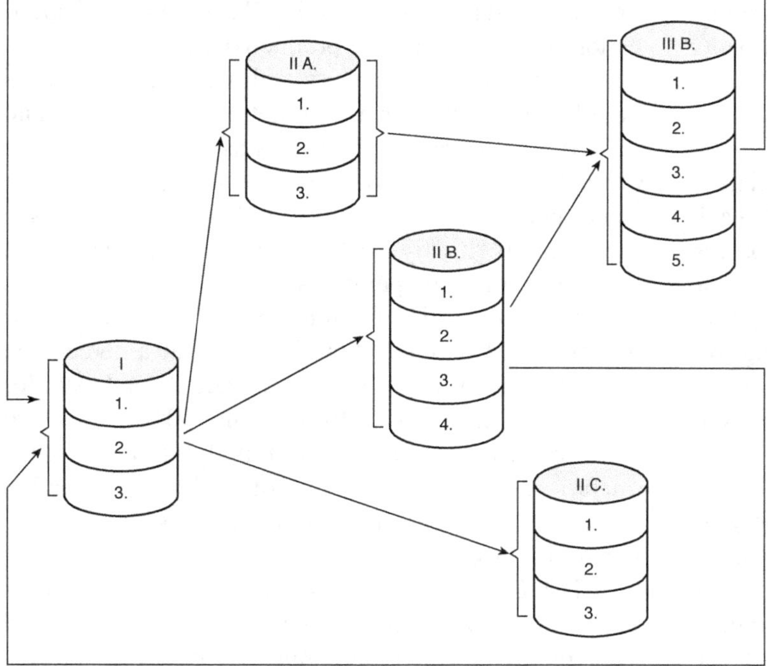

produced wealth of the national economy is produced by 100% of its available labor force. This labor force is, in turn, a portion of the total population of family (and quasi-family) households of which the total population is composed. The family household produces the new individual; so, the generic family household, as an expression of a Cantorian *Type,* is the locus of the continuing existence of the nation, and of the human species as a whole. It is the development of that family, including its new individuals, which is the proper primary referent of any sane economic policy, or economic science.

The labor force acts to produce those physical-economic changes on which depend the existence and process of continuing reproduction of the household as a whole. Thus, through the action of the labor force *as a whole,* do the households reproduce the pre-conditions for existence of that reproductive process which is the nation—mankind—*as a unit-whole.* Thus, through scientific and technological progress as a *process* of change characteristic of the cycle of labor, creative mental life, reason is the characteristic of labor and economy.

Let us now represent the bare statistical relations to be considered, using graphical diagrams and flow-lines among such bars as raw illustrations. Then, next, we return to the simple non-algebraic (e.g., cycloid) forms, to show the meaning of the apparently statistical constraints of successful growth through capital-intensive, power-intensive modes of technological progress. (See **Figures 1** and **2.**)

The successful development of an economy may be represented usefully in that statistical framework just outlined. The principles of measurement serve as a set of guidelines for bankers, statesmen, and borrowers, respecting the proportional application of sources of funds to various qualities of investment, and also as guidelines for determining the relatively more or less favorable terms and conditions associated with each class and type of loan of either national or private funds, or a mixture of both. A description of the physical-economic objectives implies the appropriate monetary, tax, and financial practice.

As we have stated in earlier chapters, the elementary function of physical economy, is the *increase of the average productive powers of labor* of the society as a whole, as measured in terms of the *variable rate of the rate of increase of potential population-density.* This mode is *capital-* and *power-intensive,* as already indicated. Within those primary terms, the conditions for growth of a physical economy can be expressed in terms of a set of *implicitly non-linear* inequalities.

Consider some relevant highlights of this practical approach to the subject-matter.

Focus now on columns I, II, and IIIb. First, take each of the columns *seriatim.*

I. Households. The rise in the level of technology requires several interrelated changes, producing a population better fed, longer lived, healthier, of higher levels of morality and culture, better educated in *science.* This requires a converging of the "school-leaving age" asymptotically upon some upper limit, approximately twenty-five years of age. This requires a longer-lived adult population, and therefore substantial increases in the ratio of senior adults (e.g., over sixty to sixty-five years of age) to total population.

This requires "smaller class size" in schools, at all levels, ever-higher levels of scientific rigor of teachers at all levels, and so on.

This requires a constant increase in the quantitative/qualitative content of the *family households* per-capita marketbasket, and increase of the quantity and raising of the cultural level of leisure.

Such are the demographic inequalities.

II. Labor Force. The total labor force of a society is a *rather* well-defined function of the family (and quasi-family) households. *Abandoned children* of working parents' working hours, are not the stuff of which sane future adults are made generally. The family supplies available wage-earners to the economy, according to a sane standard for the internal life of the child-rearing family household. That is a subject unto itself; it is sufficient, that the fact of the point's existence be noted here.

This labor force's employment must be analyzed first in respect to the total society's total relationship to nature. This relationship is defined with respect to the physical changes we recognize as physical products (such as tangible commodities of households' or pro-

ducers' consumption-marketbaskets), or as physical forms of basic economic infrastructure. These *changes* are defined functionally in respect to changes in the rate of increase of potential population-density.

The primary relationship of labor force to nature is represented by the activity of the *operatives.*

These operatives are primarily as indicated:

A. Highly skilled industrial or mining operatives, general operatives, and agricultural operatives.

B. The usefully employed *non-operatives* we defined functionally, as shown, among (1) science and engineering and related professionals, (2) education, medical, and related professionals and quasi-professionals, (3) necessary functions of administration and services, and (4) waste. By "waste," in this case, we signify employment whose form is a useful one, but whose application does not foster increase of potential population-density.

C. The category of *waste,* as distinct from wasteful employment of "non-operatives," signifies employment, or unemployment, which is intrinsically wasteful or worse in *form* per se.

These components of the total labor force, IIA and IIB, most emphatically, are applied to, distributed among, the categorical sub-sectors of IIIb. Begin analysis with IIA's distribution in terms of rations of operatives employment in each category of IIIb: (1) Infrastructure, (2) Producers' Goods, (3) Households' Goods, (4) Goods Used by Useful Forms of Administration and Services, and (5) Goods Used in Waste (wasteful applications of useful forms of productive activity).

So, in IIA, as technology and increase of potential population-density advance together, agricultural (and related) employment approaches asymptotically some ultimately "smallest possible" ration of the total labor force, perhaps in the vicinity of 1%. Simultaneously, the ration of "highly skilled operatives" increases as a percentage of total operatives.

On IIB, the ratio of employment in science and engineering professions, should increase as a percentage of total employment. Today, in the U.S.A. or Japan, for example, it *should* lie between 5 and 10% of the total labor force. This increase is principally a function of the operatives' component of the total labor force, and is associated most closely with a highly skilled component of the operatives' sector.

IIB 2. Employment of Professionals and Quasi-Professionals in Education, Medical Care, and Related Categories of Infrastructure must increase with technological progress, and with required increases in longevity, health, and productivity.

IIB 3. Employment in the growth of Administration and Services is to be constrained as much as possible. That is, the sum-total of members in the labor force employed in categories of IIA 1, 2, and 3, plus IIB 1 and 2, ought never to decline below 80 to 85% of the total labor force—in a healthy economy.

Those are the first-order data and constraining inequalities to be applied. In summary, these are:

1. There must be the indicated demographical and cultural improvements, correlating with the generation and maintenance of an increase in potential population-density by means of a continuing capital-intensive, power-intensive mode of investment in scientific and technological progress.

2. Thus the direct and indirect per-capita content of the standard family household's marketbasket must be increased in both quantity and quality, in the same correlation as demographic change.

3. Similarly, there must be a continuation of the indicated shift from rural to urban-industrial operatives' employment.

4. Similarly, within urban-industrial employment of operatives, the ration of employment in production of producers' goods (including infrastructure) must be increased relative to both total employment of operatives, *and total labor force.*

5. Similarly, the rations of employment in two sub-categories of non-operatives' employment must increase: science and engineering; and the social infra-structural sub-categories of health and education. The first should be between 5 and 10% of total employment in the U.S.A., Canada, France, Germany, Japan, etc. today. The first is keyed to technology production; the second to the correlation between technology and required shifts in demographic profiles of statistically standard family households.

These statistics, inequalities, land-use functions, and so on, correspond to a series of input-output tables, one for each historical moment of a constantly changing array of such tabular values. The result, this series of tables, is a representation of a non-linear, negentropic series of the now-familiar form, A, B, C, D, E, ... It is desired by the society which is both economically literate and sane, that the flows of credit into various sectors of the economic process cause a result corresponding to the prescribed inequalities. A sane "capitalist" economy is, like the U.S.A. under President George Washington, a nation which has rejected the British liberals' "Adam Smith's free-trade" dogma, and has chosen instead a policy akin to that of President Washington's Treasury Secretary, Alexander Hamilton. That policy is known as "the American System of Political-Economy."

The primary objective is to effect investment in advanced technologies, and that in a *physically* capital-intensive, power-intensive mode. However, to implement more advanced technology, it is indispensable to provide support in the form of expansion and technological improvements *in all dimensions of* infrastructure. That is to say, that the general advancement of technology requires:

increased water supplies per-capita and per-square-kilometer;

increased power per-capita and per-square-kilometer;

increased energy-flux density of power applied;

increased completion-rates of ton-kilometers-hours-dollars of freight moved;

better health care;

better education, and so on.

If the quality of infrastructure declines, the potential level of realized technology and productivity per-capita and per-square-kilometer declines. Now, that said, resume our comparison of the pre-Kennedy, Kennedy, and post-Kennedy "models" of economic policy.

A Rule of Thumb Approximation

Let C equal current operating costs of production-facility at 80% utilization of capacity. Let S represent the fixed investment in that capacity. Let P represent profit.

Let R equal rate of profit.

Now compare two "blackboard" cases.

$$S_1 > S_2;$$
$$C_1 = C_2; \text{ and}$$
$$R_1 > R_2.$$

However, $C_1/S_1 < C_2/S_2$.

Thus, $P_1/(C_1 + S_1) > P_2/(C_2 + S_2)$.

So, $P_1 > P_2$ by the product of $(C_1 + S_1)/(C_2 + S_2)$.

These relations exist because the investment in new technology (C_1/S_1), was based on P_1 being greater than

P_2 multiplied by the dividend of $(C_1+S_1)/(C_2+S_2)$. Although products produced by means of S_1 are probably lower in unit-price than with S_2, the higher productivity offsets this. That is the "classical" classroom-blackboard basis for the investment in S_1, rather than S_2.[2]

The Buy-back Fallacy

Years ago, United Auto Workers Union (UAW) President Walter Reuther argued, ignorantly, against automation, that machines do not buy groceries or passenger cars. This argument used by Reuther is known as the "buy-back" fallacy. The false argument runs thus. The purchasing power of a nation is the sum total of the money paid out as costs and expenses, paid-out money which becomes purchasing power. Thus, the "buy-back" argument runs, "labor-saving machinery," if it is successfully profitable, lowers the total amount of the nation's paid-out costs and expenses, and thus lowers the purchasing power of the nation. To many, that line of argument has been convincing; convincing or not, it is a falsehood, a shallow sophistry.

The margin of increase of money supply originates as a margin of credit issued. This margin of monetized credit, when redeemed by valuable goods, becomes new purchasing power in general circulation. That conversion is the key to showing the folly of the "buy-back" fallacy. It is key to the kind of monetary, tax, and financial policy which the Eisenhower administration should have followed.

The Eisenhower Case

What the Eisenhower administration did was as follows.

First, as the intensity of war-fighting in Korea was lowered to the diplomatic requirements of Panmunjon and related negotiations, the U.S. government re-enacted the essential features of the unnecessary traumatic conversion of the economy from the World War II war economy. The result was a bitter recession, roughly comparable to 1946-48 in form, although mild relative to the later Eisenhower recession and post-recession doldrums of 1957-61. What the administration then did, was to rely upon an increasingly reckless form of "consumer credit"-driven expansion of production and employment, an expansion which led, inevitably, to an early and deep collapse, into the worst postwar recession, by February-March 1957.

This short-lived, consumer credit-driven Eisenhower recovery of 1954-56 was typified by the speculative madness of the way in which retail and new car sales, and numbers of dealerships were expanded. The consumer credit-financing of these sales became a speculative financial bubble, which blew up, lawfully, inevitably, at the beginning of 1957.

Two fictions were characteristic of financial sales of new cars during that period. The first was the combined "packing" of the new-car price, and related, wild over-pricing of the allowance on the used car trade-in. The second feature *should remind us of the insanities of the 1980s real-estate boom:* the assumption that the "trade-in" value of the financed new car would enable the buyer to liquidate readily a "balloon note" concluding the series of thirty to thirty-six monthly repayment notes on the financing of the new-car sale. This latter feature was key to the triggering of the 1957 recession. During 1956 the point was being reached ever more frequently, that the unpaid balance still owed on what had been originally a new car purchase, exceeded by far the price at which an identical make and model could be purchased at a nearby used car lot.

What should have been done, instead of a consumer-credit expansion, as typified by this new car sales case, was a capital investment-led expansion. Instead of relying upon consumer-credit expansion, the Eisenhower administration should have kept consumer credit prudently tight, and focused credit-expansion into long-term investment in technologically progressive infrastructure and productive capital of, chiefly, agriculture and industry.

Instead of expanding the total consumer-goods purchasing power by increasingly reckless consumer short- to medium-term indebtedness, the administration should have increased total consumer purchasing power by means of the higher per-capita wage levels of technologically progressive capital expansion. It is the increase of the total households' cash pay envelope purchasing power, through the combination of job expansion and skill-related employment upgrading, which is the proper basis for a durable growth of the households' goods market.

Interestingly, the Eisenhower folly on this account was the General Motors folly. Henry Ford had conceived the automobile as a household's long-term in-

---

2. That is merely a rule-of-thumb approximation; the correct function considers the effect of the choice of investment-allotment upon the rate of return consequently realized by the economy as a whole. That is, the sum of the optimal profits of the aggregate firms of an economy, does not define the profitability of the economy as a whole.

vestment medium in a capital good of a household/farm. Christiania/Wall Street-linked General Motors had introduced the sweat-shop ideology of the New York City Seventh Avenue garment-manufacturing industry into automobile marketing, and thus, into automotive manufacturing. Robert Strange McNamara was the instrument to introduce the "Seventh Avenue sweatshop" mentality to Ford Motor Company operations.

The difference in the two approaches may be illustrated as follows:

The "Seventh Avenue," or "horizontal" approach of General Motors style-season marketing, which Wall Street's "loony" Robert Strange McNamara carried into the politically defeated Ford Motor Company of the 1950s, is in direct opposition to the "verticality" of the sane, industrial approach. The industrial approach changes the composition of total corporate and sales products, to increase the relative portion of high-technology producers' goods. It is this relative expansion of producers' goods production and sales, which increases both the scale and per-capita incomes of industrial employment, thus avoiding the horizontal approach's tendency to seek a speculative boom based upon misused consumer credit mechanisms.

To illustrate this important point, take the case of hypothetical automotive manufacturer "A." With technological progress, "A's" passenger vehicles divisions produce an increased volume of units, of improved quality, with a reduction in operatives in all these divisions combined. Shall this lead to a corresponding margin of increased unemployment among the employees of "A"? Not if the sane industrial approach is employed.

The normal line of promotion within the ranks of operatives in an integrated aerospace/automotive enterprise (such as "A" should be) is from "the general operative," toward machine-tool specialist, and so on. If "A" takes the industrial approach indicated, this firm coordinates technological advances in its passenger vehicles divisions with increasing production and marketing of classes of capital goods cohering with its overall technological requirements.

A sound such enterprise should employ about 5% or more of its total operatives force in research and development, or should support an outside research and development vendor to supply such an effect.

Government plays a critical role in shaping the economy on this account.

First, government at various levels (federal, state, county) either builds and operates the needed basic economic infrastructure, or provides regulation of privately owned public utilities to the same net effect. This investment is a large component of the nation's total long-term, productive capital investment, and is the most important such investment—upon which the feasibility of every other investment depends.

The production of currently and foreseeably needed capital improvements in basic economic infrastructure, is the proper, principal "driver" in increases of both total employment and per-capita productivity. The same is true of capital- and power-intensive investments in improved technology, generally.

Imagine an entire economy analogous to the enterprise "A," above. As technological progress enables us to produce a higher per-capita value of households' consumption marketbasket with a smaller fraction of the total labor force than earlier, instead of shunting the redundant margin of operatives into the ranks of the unemployed, or useless low-paid services employments, this margin should be absorbed by job upgrading, into the domain of capital goods production.

Thus, if the new issues of U.S. currency notes authorized by Congress are entrusted for lending to a national bank such as Hamilton's or Biddle's United States Bank, the following practice is to be desired.

The national bank may lend these notes either directly to borrowers, or the loan may be issued, in cooperation with the national bank, by a private member-bank of the national banking system as a whole.

Generally, federal, state, county, and municipal infrastructural agencies would prefer to borrow directly from the national bank. In federal cases, this would be the rule. Private agencies would usually borrow through a private member-bank of the national system; customarily, the private bank would supply a significant portion of the total credit issued.

The chief purposes of national bank lending as a whole are two. First, to supply low-price, long-term credit for capital improvements in basic economic infrastructure, and second, to foster optimal realization of the private sector's capacity to absorb new productive capital formation in connection with agriculture, mining, and manufacturing:

• in publicly owned basic infrastructure, the national bank is the chief source of such credit *for capital improvements*;

• in public utilities, national banking credit may be a major contributor of lines of such credit when the specific circumstances warrant this;

• in agriculture and mining, the national bank is a significant indirect lender;

• in the manufacturing sector, the national bank is a significant participant in capital loans which foster those kinds of capital-intensive, power-intensive investments in technological progress which have the relatively greatest beneficial impact upon the economy as a whole.

Since the new circulation of U.S. currency notes is, in these cases, always tied to a corresponding increase in physical wealth produced, there is no inflationary impact in lending in a manner analogous to progressively issued construction notes. In the degree that lending fosters capital- and power-intensive modes of investment in technological progress, that impact is *deflationary.*

Thus, technological progress effected so, means an expansion of the scale of the economy's per-capita output. The monetary support for this marginal expansion of scale of product produced and sold, is properly supplied by the national banking mechanism, in accordance with provisions within Article I of the U.S. Constitution.

Eisenhower and the Fourth Republic

Earlier here, we said that it would be useful to see similarities in the contrast between Kennedy and Eisenhower, in the one case, and between President Charles de Gaulle and the French Fourth (and Third) Republics, in another case.

Under the leadership of King Louis XI, France was not only re-created as the first modern form of nation-state republic, but as a leading economy as well. Under Mazarin's protégé Minister Jean-Baptiste Colbert, France became the world's leading nation in science, technology, and economy, until 1815. Although the followers of Descartes undermined France's eighteenth-century science, and although the Jacobin terror sought to literally decapitate French science, over the period of 1793-1814, Lazare Carnot and his collaborator Gaspard Monge revived science and kept France in first rank until the Bourbon Restoration. Thus, the relative scientific and technological stagnation which dominated French history from 1815 until de Gaulle's Fifth Republic, is an uncharacteristic feature of modern French history and culture taken as a whole, if the entirety of the span from the fifteenth-century accession of Louis XI is taken into account.

The problem of France's Second, Third, and Fourth Republics can be summed up in a word, "Buggery": the Bugger-like, Rosicrucian philosophical world outlook of a powerful rentier financial interest centered historically around that Baron James Rothschild so bitterly described by the great Heinrich Heine, the France whose rentier corruption is so famously described by participant Honoré Balzac. That is the characteristic tendency of *rentier* Wall Street's Eisenhower administration—the United States mimicking the charlatan's empire of France's Napoleon III.

Thus notable differences aside, Kennedy's bold policy reforms in economy are an escape from the intellectual morass of the Eisenhower 1950s, an escape paralleling de Gaulle's rescue of France from the moral miasma of the Fourth Republic.

As President de Gaulle recognized in practice, the right agro-industrial program must fail, if it does not include a vigorous, leading science-driver component. Three elements of the Kennedy recovery program were *indispensable:*

I. Acceleration of development of basic economic infrastructure.

II. Fostering power-intensive, capital-intensive investment in productivity increases, through an investment tax-credit program.

III. Taking on the Federal Reserve System, in defense of the U.S. Constitution. (President Kennedy in mid-1963 ordered the drafting of an Executive Order, which explicitly ordered the Federal Reserve to cease the practice of creation of U.S. currency by Federal Reserve action in rediscounting of Treasury notes. The order would have left the Treasury solely authorized to issue currency of the United States, as required by the Constitution. The assassination of Kennedy intervened before he promulgated the order, and it was never recurred to by subsequent Presidents.)

One additional feature was *essential*:

IV. Demanding Moon landing as a science driver for the economy as a whole.

Without technological progress, in a capital-intensive, power-intensive mode, there is no substantial growth of sustainable improvement in productivity. It is essential to bring monetary, tax, financial, and economic regulatory policy into conformity with that principle. So, these four, and correlated features of the Kennedy economic recovery represented, without fear of exaggeration, a revolutionary "cultural paradigm-shift," away from the "Fourth Republic-like" moral and intellectual decadence of the "baby boomer"-vintage Eisenhower decade. Kennedy's economic policy was a revolutionary shift, away from a rentier, toward a "Hamiltonian" practice.

Unfortunately, if the Eisenhower decade was a purgatory of moral and intellectual decadence, the counter-revolution unleashed by the November 1963 assassination of President Kennedy, was purely a Crowleyite, Nietzschean, Dionysiac Hell.

The Credit System

Under the British central banking system, or our U.S. Federal Reserve System, for example, a financial oligarchy exerts a usurious dictatorship over the nation's money supply. Under such systems, which originate in ancient Babylonian tax-farming, the state issues money by either collection of money as taxes, or borrowing advance payments from private holders of nominal wealth in their capacity as tax-farmers.

The only significant alternatives to this dictatorial rule by oligarchy are two: (1) that the state outlaw usury as a capital crime; (2) that the state, or an alliance between state and benign agro-industrial interests, provide an alternative to the oligarchic, usurious forms of tax-farming and central banking. The best alternative developed thus far, is the American System of national credit and banking.

All economic theory and practice is divided principally into two types: (1) the doctrine that wealth flows from the borrowing and circulation of an original hoard of money; (2) the opposing view that the origin of wealth is production, and that money is merely a means of fostering the circulation of that produced wealth.

Under President George Washington's American System, to which this report proposes we return, two forms of banking enjoy a cooperative existence to their mutual advantage. The one form of banking is "Hamilton's" national banking; the other, is the entrepreneurial, usually state-chartered, regulated system of private banking institutions. In this division of labor, the power to create *currency (legal tender)* is absolutely a monopoly of the federal government, as provided under the relevant terms of Article I of the U.S. Constitution. The division of labor is, summarily, as follows:

1. The President of the United States requests from the federal Congress, a bill authorizing the Secretary of the Treasury to create and circulate a specified issue of United States non-interest-bearing currency notes as legal tender.

2. The U.S. Treasury might place such newly issued notes into circulation as cash payments for federal government purchases or payroll on current operating account. It is preferred, by far, that all payments on account of federal government operations be paid from sums accrued as paid-in tax revenues and tariffs.

3. The preferred, customary method of introducing a new issue of currency notes into general circulation is through lending. Two channels for lending might be employed: loans issued directly by the U.S. Treasury, or loans issued against new currency issues which have been placed on deposit with a chartered bank of the United States.

4. Loans issued by a chartered bank of the United States are properly restricted by guidelines, which, in turn, are established according to statute, by an executive order of the President. These guidelines cover all non-emergency loans issued by that bank, as follows:

The functional classes of borrowing agencies are broadly defined by aid of a cross-grid of three classifications, each with associated subordinate elements, as seen in **Figure 3**:

Consider the following, brief illustrations:

The urgent national freshwater development needs of the U.S.A. are reflected chiefly by a combination of one major project, an expanded NAWAPA (North American Water and Power Alliance) project, plus a policy of fostering state-of-the-art desalination applications and other water-treatment programs of localized application. A very large percentage of total U.S. water development investment during the coming fifteen to twenty years is represented by that package. Similarly, the largest single component of *new* national transportation investment during the coming two decades, is represented by a modernized nationwide railway network, featuring high-speed friction-rail (principally for freight) and magnetic levitation (initially, principally for intra-urban, suburban, and long-range passenger travel).

In the case of major power-generation expansion, we have also a clear—if presently controversial—choice. The only practicable sources of major power supply during the coming hundred years are nuclear fission and nuclear fusion. This should be used for the following principal applications: electrical power, industrial and other process heat, water management, and production of hydrogen and related fuels for internal-combustion and analogous vehicles. And so on, for infrastructure. A few major, national projects, and dove-

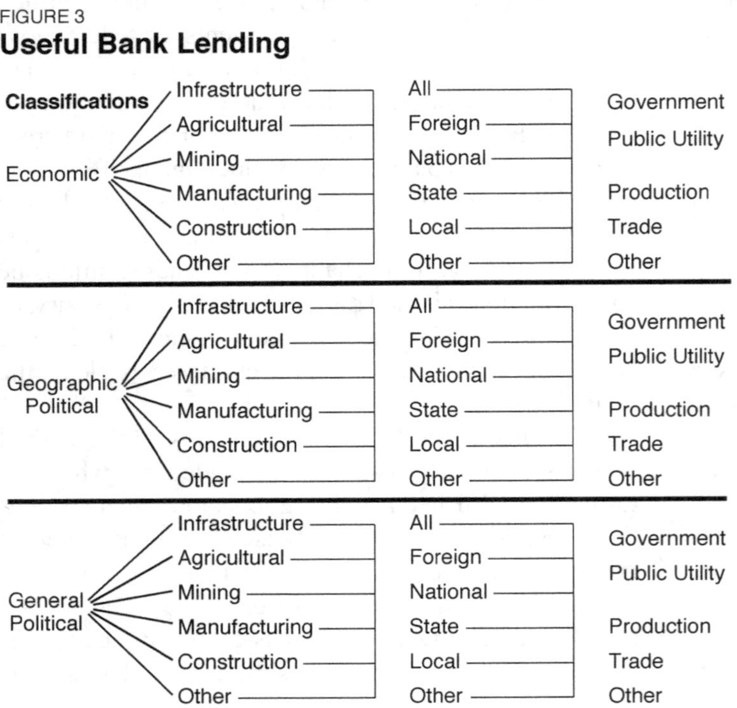

tailing state and local programs, cover most classes of national need over the next generation. The relationship of these programs to potential productive investment in population support is fairly described as "calculable." Also, the manpower and other resources required for each of these projects is estimable by any relevant consortium of engineering firms.

Similarly, it is feasible to calculate the impact of such projects upon the economy. The "draw-down" of available labor force is calculable, and also of materials and other semi-finished and finished producers' goods. The impact of the increased monetary purchasing power generated by relevant margins of increased sales of households' and producers' goods, is thus also calculable. Also, the increase of the federal, state, and local tax revenue bases is calculable. Those increases in gross monetary purchasing power and tax revenues ought to be applied in proportions consistent with the constraints (non-linear inequalities) consistent with real growth. Such a latter effect can be fostered *indirectly* through the marginal effects of proportional allotments of lendable new issue of legal tender through the private banks of the national banking system.

The nation as a whole is divided into its obvious economic regions, as groups of states. The loan officers of the chartered national bank, are supplied with "flex-ible budget" guidelines for loan-participations by type and by state within region. The loan officers are the channel through which member private banks conduct business respecting participation of the chartered national bank (e.g., a U.S. Bank) in lending programs.

Those, in rough sketch-form, are the outlines of the system.

The national bank is engaged in medium- to long-term lending, and only by exception in short-term lending. Most of the loans' value lies within two categories: principal lending-support for designated projects; or sub-categories such as public utilities' capital improvements.

The proper economic functions of non-usurious banking, from this vantage-point, are typified by examining three types: (1) the indicated type of chartered national bank; (2) the savings bank; and (3) the commercial bank, this latter the usual partner in the national bank's loan-participation programs. It is the distinctive function of the latter type which is now scrutinized.

The economic function of the commercial bank lies within what is fairly described as its "lending based upon a prudent assessment of business risk." This function is derived historically from such precedents as Tudor England's issuance of patents of temporary monopoly to inventors and their business partners in ventures producing and marketing that invention. Thus, consider only notions of "business risk" cohering with the effective production and marketing of a useful improvement in technology. Consider, from this standpoint, the proper division of economic responsibility between government and the entrepreneur.

For example, no sane nation would allow its military or law-enforcement agencies, or courts, to be delegated to a private enterprise. In the case of law-enforcement agencies or courts, "privatization" is transparently a form of *corruption per se*. We cannot leave it to the private entrepreneurship to decide whether some communities in the nation do, or do not have adequate public transportation, fresh water, power, and so forth. However, at the opposite pole, we could not permit the majority of the citizenry or government to decide upon what useful ideas will be allowed to be fostered in general communications, or in the marketplace. It is the history of mankind, that the most useful conceptions, upon which the existence of modern society significantly depends, came into practice as the opinion of a relatively tiny group, or even a nearly isolated single person.

Indeed, the fact that all valid scientific discovery depends originally upon the sovereign authority of an individual mind's mental-creative processes, signals the necessity of certain classes of individual entrepreneurship for human progress, and hence continued existence in general. Some societies may disagree with that view; if they persist in such an opinion, they will be ultimately destroyed, as communist society is being self-destroyed before our eyes today.

There is a middle ground, between those matters in which government must intervene, to promote definite directions in scientific and technological progress, and, at the opposite pole, areas to which the principles of free speech are rightly extended, to preclude government interference. The middle ground, is that into which government may or may not choose to intervene, and may do so whenever reason shows this to be more than merely desirable;

1. Government must, of course, demand a minimal level of competence in pre-science and science in public education. Witchcraft is not to be tolerated as a substitute for geometry.

2. Government must support scientific research to the degree obligations of government cannot be adequately fulfilled otherwise. The current HIV pandemic illustrates this point. Beginning 1985-86, the federal government lied officially about the dangers of what is called today HIV infection, because, as Surgeon General Koop and others argued, the federal government did not wish to be panicked into new massive expenditures under the then-prevailing conditions of major budget crisis. Saving Gramm-Rudman was considered more important than saving human lives. How many people have died, or will die, avoidably, because of the callously inhuman decision by the federal government then? The proposal for a colonization of Mars, is another example of this issue. Fifty, sixty, and more years ahead, our posterity will face challenges which they could not solve, unless we begin an appropriate Mars colonization "crash project" now.

3. The cases of the Manhattan Project, President de Gaulle's successful, "dirigist" approach to the development of France's Fifth Republic, and a highly profitable Kennedy "Moon-landing" aerospace program, illustrate the kinds of large-scale, ostensibly optional, government "crash science-oriented programs" which sound governments will always be seeking out.

Otherwise, as indicated, government bears the responsibility for arranging the supply and maintenance of an adequate per-capita and per-square-kilometer's development of basic economic infrastructure for the territory and population of the nation as a whole. This includes the element of mandatory, not optional technological progress, and also the scale and capital-intensity of that investment.

To appreciate adequately the nature of a proper prohibition against government interference, we must strictly define the term "freedom," to equate "freedom" with creative powers of reason, as "creative reason" is defined in preceding chapters of this report. In this instance, the economic issue of science policy assumes the form of the proposition: What must government not leave, by its own omission, to the functions of individual entrepreneurs; and where must government not interfere with freedom of scientific inquiry and advocacy by a person, groups of persons, and business entrepreneurships?

It is the duty of government to foster, and to defend, a policy of capital-intensive, power-intensive productive investment in scientific and technological progress, as the general policy of the nation. This duty of government is expressed ordinarily in the form of development and maintenance of a well-regulated system of infrastructure, of national banking, and of taxation policies. This ordinary expression is properly supplemented by long-term so-called "science-driver" projects.

The Newton-versus-Leibniz controversy, continuing into the present time, is a prime illustration of a related problem of national science policy. Western European civilization, and now most of the nations of this planet, depend for their existence upon at least a certain minimal level of technology of general practice, and also a certain, at least minimal rate of scientific and technological progress in connection with that general practice. Thus, it would be criminal, in effect, for any government to proceed in opposition to scientific and technological progress. Thus, since we must reject as insane and immoral all anti-science policies per se, we are left with the kinds of disputes typified by the continuing Newton-Leibniz controversy.

In this matter of the Newton-Leibniz issue, to the degree that government knows that Leibniz's views are relatively the correct ones, to what degree must we permit Newtonians, for example, the prerogatives of "protected free speech"? Shall we, therefore, tolerate the peddler who sells strychnine, atropine, opium, and mycotoxin as "natural foods"? When do we come near to the obligation to prohibit poisonous ideas of such or kindred quality? These are not easy questions to answer rightly; other matters of principle must be considered first. We shall lay the basis for doing so, after summarizing the successive disasters of the past twenty-eight years of post-Kennedy U.S. economic and related policy-shaping.

After Kennedy

The assassination of President Kennedy coincided with the unleashing of an interacting set of prepared economic, financial, monetary, and cultural changes in the axiomatics of public morality—a "cultural paradigm-shift." Taken as a whole, these axiomatic changes are fairly grouped under the "New Age" rubric.

1. *In economics:* a shift away from a rising standard of productivity and household life, based upon fostering scientific and technological progress, toward the utopia of a "neo-Malthusian post-industrial society."

2. *In finance:* a shift toward deregulation and unbridled financial speculation, premised upon the unfettered practice of usury.

3. *In monetary affairs:* an end to the gold reserve basis, and stable currencies of the postwar Bretton Woods agreements, in favor of a usurious speculator's "floating exchange-rate" system.

4. *In cultural affairs:* a combination of the satanic (Dionysiac) rock-drug-sex counterculture, with kindred effluent of the Theodor Adorno "Frankfurt School" and Brigadier John Rawlings Rees's London Tavistock Clinic.

Case in point: The Johnson administration proposed to take down the Kennedy aerospace program significantly, on the pretext of freeing money "from space" for "the war on poverty" at home. This hoax, known as the Great Society, plunged the darker-complected minorities, on the average, successively, notch by notch, lower down on the socio-economic ladder, while also bringing to an end the genuine economic growth generated by the Kennedy crash aerospace program.

This change, cutting aerospace savagely, had been recommended to the Johnson administration by the London Tavistock Institute's Rapoport report on the effects of the Kennedy aerospace crash program. The burden of the Rapoport report: Aerospace was capturing the imagination of the majority of the population, was fostering greater admiration for scientific achieve-

ments, and was having the undesired (by Tavistock) effect of promoting a spread of increased rationality within the U.S. population. The aerospace program was promptly set back.

Case in point: Wrecking Bretton Woods came in six successive phases.

Phase 1: Johnson's mid-1960s slashing of aerospace fostered a serious recession. This played into the London-orchestrated collapse of the British pound and the U.S. dollar, over the November 1967-November 1968 interval.

Phase 2: Dragging that imbecilic quality of economic illiteracy known as the "free trade" dogmas of Professor Milton Friedman (and later, Prime Minister Margaret Thatcher) into the White House, with the newly elected President Nixon, ensured the 1970-71 collapses which behind-the-scenes plotters used to maneuver Nixon into wrecking the last remains of the Bretton Woods gold-reserve agreements, and plunging the world into the accelerating spiral of speculative-inflationary orgy known euphemistically as "the floating exchange-rate system."

Phase 3: The Kissinger oil-price hoax of 1973-75.

The first, 1972 outbreak of the scandal surrounding the Kissinger-created "White House plumbers' unit" assisted Kissinger in aiding London to unleash "a new Middle East war," and to set up Secretary of State Rogers later to be dumped in favor of Kissinger's appointment to hold Rogers's job, in addition to his original post at the National Security Council. This enabled Kissinger's masters in London and Kissinger himself to orchestrate the famous "oil-price hoax" of the mid-1970s. This shock caused more serious immediate damage to the world economy than the 1970-71 monetary crisis. In fact, the effects of the oil-price hoax were used by London and London's agent Kissinger, to shape the new monetary agreements established at the 1975 Rambouillet monetary conference.

Phase 4: The "Project 1980s" plan for "controlled disintegration of the economy."

This project was prepared during the 1975-76 interval at the New York branch of Kissinger's London (Chatham House) masters, the New York Council of Foreign Relations. The papers were assembled under the direction of future Secretary of State Cyrus Vance and future National Security Adviser Zbigniew Brzezinski. The Carter administration carried out the policies of these papers, including the 1979 appointment of a Federal Reserve chairman, the Paul A. Volcker who announced that he regarded "controlled disintegration of the economy" as an acceptable policy.

Phase 5: Deregulation of banking and transportation.

Circa 1978, the Carter administration moved to bankrupt the nation's prosperous airlines and trucking industries, and many smaller communities of the nation, by pushing deregulation through the Congress. Today, we observe the results of that. Banking deregulation, the key to the 1980s wipe-out of the nation's S&Ls, and of the leading commercial banks, too, was set into motion in 1978, by the proposal to allow the Hongkong and Shanghai Bank to take over the New York-based Marine Midland Bank.

The issue of the HongShang takeover was essentially this. By allowing the drug-money-laundering banking system of the British Commonwealth's "offshore" zones to take over U.S. banks without full audit transparency, the Carter administration, and Federal Reserve Chairman Volcker, opened up the U.S.A. not only for full-scale flood of illegal narcotics, but a takeover of our financial system by the financial institutions behind the Asian and South American drug-lords. It happened, just as this writer and his associates warned back in 1978 and 1979.

Phase 6: 1982 Deregulation.

The last major phase of the collapse of the U.S. economy was set into motion in 1982. Once that year had ended, certainly by the summer of 1983, the U.S. banking system was doomed to plunge into successive waves of bankruptcy, with ultimate results for the entire banking system, and the economy as a whole, far worse than President Herbert Hoover's Great Depression of the early 1930s. By the second half of 1987, a new depression was in full swing.

August-October 1982 was the last chance to save the U.S. banking system in its then-existing institutional form. On that issue, this writer was on the front line, trying to save the banking system which did not seem to wish to be saved from its own acts of mass-suicide down the road.

During the months of June and August 1982, this writer produced a book-length special report, entitled *Operation Juárez,* which was delivered at the beginning of August that year. This report had been prepared at the May-June request of certain key officials of Central American and South American governments, as an action package for the case of a financial blowout which the writer had forecast to hit Mexico and other states no

EIRNS/Stuart Lewis

Henry A. Kissinger. "So long as the lunatic Kissinger and Bush financial policies of 1982 remain in force, the U.S. financial system must continue to fly ever nearer to the precipice."

later than September 1982.

In August 1982, the crisis struck as this reporter had forecast throughout the preceding months. For several hours, approximately, the international financial system hovered at the precipice of a global chain-reaction collapse. U.S. President Ronald Reagan's telephone conversation with Mexico's President José López Portillo arranged stop-gap action to delay the crisis.

Mexico's President acted at home, taking first steps along the lines proposed by *Operation Juárez.* Unfortunately, under pressure from a savage gang led by former U.S. Secretary of State and British foreign intelligence agent Henry A. Kissinger, the governments of Argentina and Brazil withdrew their backing for Mexico. Kissinger flew to Mexico, to meet with President López Portillo and his successor, Miguel de la Madrid. The measures which could have saved Mexico from usurious looting by Kissinger's fellow hyenas were terminated. The collapse of the U.S. banking system, which *Operation Juárez* would have prevented, was merely postponed, and made inevitable.

A U.S. Congress apparently gone mad rammed through support for the policies of Kissinger and for the insane banking deregulation measures supported by then-Vice President George Bush. So, as long as the lunatic Kissinger and Bush financial policies of 1982 remained in force, the U.S. financial system must continue to fly ever-nearer to the precipice. Beyond that is no mere depression-level financial collapse, nothing relatively as mild as Hoover's Great Depression of the 1930s. What is now visibly in progress, already at the verge of terminal collapse, is a disintegration of most among the principal financial institutions of the Anglo-American financial system—worldwide.

Since that autumn of 1982, we have already experienced the spring 1984 banking crisis, the October 1987 collapse, the 1988-90 collapse of those eaten-out carcasses which remained of the pre-1979 savings and loan industry, and now, a growing roster of leading financial institutions which are "brain dead" relics maintained solely by the Bush administration's taxpayer-funded life-support system.

The Intellectual Decay of Management

The mayfly celebrity of a dangerous idiot, Harvard University's economics professor Jeffrey Sachs, is, like a fresh, epidemic outbreak of herpes, a sign of a deep, perhaps mortal mental illness pervading the currently reigning "yuppie" generation of Anglo-American economic life. The quality of competence we associated with high-performance industrial-corporate management as recently as the early seventies, is past retirement age. Their replacements in top posts, during the late 1970s, were, on the average, intellectually inferior in every way; the next wave of promotions following that, during the middle to late 1980s, was chiefly pathetic by comparison with all predecessors. Sachs, and his milieu at Harvard, MIT, and elsewhere, typify the very worst results of this pathetic, downward trend in mental and moral qualities.

The nature of this mental and moral decay is typified not only by the phenomenon of a vicious ignoramus like Sachs; prior to the late 1970s, only a handful of querulous economics illiterates would have been duped into admiring something as banally fraudulent as Professor Milton Friedman's "Free To Choose" television series. In a saner time, when average concentration-span was significantly longer, the babbling of Britain's former Prime Minister Margaret Thatcher would not have been tolerated.

We have to consider not only the malignant, dangerous illiteracy of a Professor Sachs; we must account for the dismal intellectual level of a relevant public opinion which tolerates such obvious rubbish as Sach's "shock therapy."

At first inspection, the cause of this collapse in the intellectual quality of our population has been neither genetic nor accidental. In short, the cause is "Buggery," perpetrated by "Buggers" ranging from William James and John Dewey, through Bertrand Russell, H.G. Wells, the American Family Foundation's roots in MK-Ultra, Brigadier John Rawlings Rees's London Tavistock Clinic network, and the Communist International project of subversion commonly known as Theodor Adorno's and Hannah Arendt's "Frankfurt School." The names of the projects by which the intellect and morals of the U.S. population were intentionally destroyed, include Hollywood, the "Radio Research Project," "soap opera," and the "rock-drug-sex counterculture," the "new math," "sensitivity training," and related mass-brainwashing modes.

This destruction of a large margin of the previously existing intellectual powers, and moral qualities of so large and widespread a ration of the post-1963 youth generations of the U.S. population, has been the explicitly intended result in a process of cultural subversion which began much earlier than CIA director Allen Dulles's adoption of a British intelligence-directed, mass-brainwashing project known by such official names as "MK-Ultra." The forerunners of MK-Ultra include such Communist International-designed subversion projects as the "Frankfurt School" of Theodor Adorno, Hannah Arendt et al., and also, related to the "Frankfurt School" the center of satanic orgies known as the mobster-directed Hollywood film and TV production colony. The 1963 launching of the mass-recruitment phase of the Tavistock-linked, Crowleyite, rock-drug-sex counterculture had roots older than the freemasonic "Young America" cult of satanic Giuseppe Mazzini and that treasonous degenerate Albert Pike.

The reader of approximately forty years of age or older, is aware of the greatness of the degree to which the average levels of mere literacy, concentration span, knowledge, and morality have collapsed during the past twenty-eight years. Twenty-eight years ago, an ideological quack such as recent British Prime Minister Thatcher would have been rightly classed in the same general category as Uganda's Idi Amin. A silly, but dangerous fascist, such as Harvard University economics professor Jeffrey Sachs, would have caused the scandal-ridden collapse of any U.S. administration caught sponsoring such a wretch, as the Bush administration has imposed Sachs upon looted, defenseless Poland.

More and more, as the older generation dies out, hastened to "death with dignity" by the greedy heirs called their "baby boomer" generation offspring, the intellectual, cultural, and moral level of the U.S. population has sunk lower and then yet lower. That population, ever more ignorant, ever more suggestible, ever more "other-directed," has succumbed more or less passively, to an ever-worsening pattern of atrocities in conditions of life, and in the Washington policies which foster those horrors. To read the daily newspapers and other popular periodicals of the day, to survey the preferred TV "news" and other mass entertainments, is to see so reflected the banality, ignorance, moral indifference, and worse qualities which the past quarter-century's *directed* "cultural paradigm-shift" has induced in the majority of the population. Is this, perhaps, a population which shows itself thus, to be a nation which has lost the moral fitness to survive? Is such a people capable of both recognizing and adopting those specific, radical changes in both popular and governmental behavior which are indispensable to the medium-term survival of the United States in its present institutional form?

The famous, thread-bare aphorism is, "whom the gods would destroy, they first make mad." In truth, whom the Satanists would destroy, they first seduce into destroying themselves. It is the same thing, in appearance, in the end. Your greatest enemy sits there staring at you, luring you to your mind's self-destruction; it is your television set. That television set, and the imagined countercultural pleasures which it symbolizes, is your fatal, Faustian pact with Satan.

Satan Sells 'Junk Bonds'

Your pension has been stolen. It was stolen by a set of accomplices which includes President George Bush's cronies at Kohlberg Kravis Roberts, and which includes such Hollywood-styled news-media celebrities and predators as Ivan Boesky and Michael Milken. The way it happened is typified by the following actual case, featuring KKR and Minnesota State Attorney General Hubert "Skip" Humphrey III.

The prelude to this unpleasant little true story occurs during the late 1970s, when Washington decided to take the pension funds out of the control of wicked unions, and put them under "professional" management. Next step, loot the pension funds, swapping relatively solid securities for "junk bonds." The junk-bond scam hit the big time, when KKR and others discovered the way to loot pension funds, unloading junk bonds in the way a batch of this was dumped on Minnesota by courtesy of watchdog "Skip" Humphrey.

"Junk bonds" is a name with an historically appropriate ring of irony to it. During the 1968-82 interval, neo-Malthusian ideologues such as Zbigniew Brzezinski and James R. Schlesinger transformed our once-envied agro-industrial power into a wasting heap of obsolescent, "post-industrial" rubble. Out of this rubble came the worst pestilence of sociopathic financial predators since the fourteenth-century House of Bardi's scalawags, Biche and Mouche. The "Burkes and Hares" of modern financial parasitism,45 such as Kravis, Boesky, and Milken, brought the business ethics of the "resurrection man" to such forms of legalized theft as "hostile takeover" and "leveraged buyout."

This business of "junk bonds," and similar forms of wildly fictitious financial wealth, compares unfavorably with the John Law speculative bubbles of the early eighteenth century. It is fairly described as mass insanity. It is the essence of what the Thatcherite 1980s came to signify by such yuppie catch phrases as "deregulation" and "free trade."

Back in the period 1966-73, when this writer was teaching a one-semester course in economics at various locations, one of the standard "professor's jokes" which crept into my lecture routine, concerned the ideal business firm of the so-called "technetronic age." Unfortunately, as years have passed since I last taught that course, in spring 1973, the reality has come to resemble that old joke.

I projected the trend of shifts in rations of employment, away from "blue collar" productive jobs, toward larger and larger proportions of employment in nonproductive forms of low-skilled administration and services. If this trend, combined with merger trends, were to continue, one might imagine a not-too-distant time when all U.S. production was concentrated in a single firm, housed in a giant skyscraper, above ground, floor after floor filled with sales offices, executive suites, legions of clerks, and data-processing. The firm's production would be concentrated in the basement, where a single little old man, using a simple craftsman's tools, turned out daily the whole product administered by the occupants of the floors above.

What happens to the U.S. economy on the day that little old man retires, I used to ask.

Naturally, it is 1991, and the U.S. economy is not yet near that extreme; millions are still employed in productive "blue collar" jobs in agriculture, mining, manufacturing, and infrastructure. So, like most good jokes (and poor ones, too), I exaggerated a bit at the lectern. Yet, things were going in that direction, and now they have gone far enough that the economy is collapsing as a result.

1966-67's turn toward a hoax called the 'Great Society" was a step in the direction of Robert M. Hutchins' *Triple Revolution* utopia. That was the first giant step downward in the direction pioneered by the ruinous British government of Prime Minister Harold Wilson. The 1967-68 wrecking of the original Bretton Woods agreements, and the later, 1971-72 scrapping of the indispensable gold-reserve arrangement, were giant steps downward.

The introduction of "environmentalism" and of "New Age" educational reforms, was a slippery road toward national bankruptcy. Secretary of State (and British agent) Henry A. Kissinger's 1973-74 petroleum-price hoax, was another major step down. The Carter administration was an economic and financial disaster from beginning to end, but all done under the direction of the "Project 1980s" package created by the real, Council on Foreign Relations creators and controllers of the Carter-Mondale administration. The two worst blows to the economy under Carter, were the launching of "deregulation" of transportation and banking, and the unleashing of newly appointed Federal Reserve Chairman Paul A. Volcker's policy of "controlled disintegration of the economy" in October 1979.

Nineteen eighty-two was the year of crucial decisions. The Reagan administration entered a deadly financial crisis during summer 1982, with my *Operation Juárez* on one side of the desk, and the wildly speculative looting policies of Walter Wriston, Henry Kissinger, and George Bush, on the opposite side. When my policies were turned down, the U.S. financial and monetary system was doomed to collapse hopelessly a relative few years down the line.

There we are at the brink, today.

FIDELIO

Journal of Poetry, Science, and Statecraft

From the first issue, dated Winter 1992, featuring Lyndon LaRouche on "The Science of Music: The Solution to Plato's Paradox of 'The One and the Many,'" to the final issue of Spring/Summer 2006, a "Symposium on Edgar Allan Poe and the Spirit of the American Revolution," *Fidelio* magazine gave voice to the Schiller Institute's intention to create a new Golden Renaissance.

The title of the magazine, is taken from Beethoven's great opera, which celebrates the struggle for political freedom over tyranny. *Fidelio* was founded at the time that LaRouche and several of his close associates were unjustly imprisoned, as was the opera's Florestan, whose character was based on the American Revolutionary hero, the French General, Marquis de Lafayette.

Each issue of *Fidelio*, throughout its 14-year lifespan, remained faithful to its initial commitment, and offered original writings by LaRouche and his associates, on matters of, what the poet Percy B* Byssche Shelley identified as, "profound and impassioned conceptions respecting man and nature."

Back issues are now available for purchase through the Schiller Institute website:
http://schillerinstitute.org/about/order_form.html

II. The Power To Change History

Great Opportunity—Great Danger

LaRouche PAC Nationwide Fireside Chat with Will Wertz (edited) of Aug, 24, 2017

Moderator Lynne Speed of Mahattan opened the call.

Will Wertz: Okay, thank you Lynne. I think you have to look at this moment in history in the way that the German poet, dramatist and historian, Friedrich Schiller, looked at the period of the French Revolution. He wrote a short two-line poem shortly after the French Revolution, called, "The Moment"; and it goes as follows: "A momentous epoch has the century engendered. Yet the moment so great findeth a people so small." And that's the challenge before us at this point in history: to overcome smallness of mind—not to be taken in by infantile fixations, to put it in those terms. We are at a situation where we have potential to move forward for a common destiny of all humanity. President Trump's election, particularly in certain key areas, represents the potential for the United States to join in this grand strategy for humanity. And as Lynne Speed just mentioned, there are especially two areas which are critical. First of all, he rejected the entire policy of regime-change, which we've been involved in—perpetual warfare—over the last couple of decades, especially under George W. Bush and then under President Obama. He rejected the war in Iraq; he criticized heavily the effort in Libya, which resulted in the assassination of President Qaddafi; he has moved, although slowly in a certain sense because of the attack on him for his alleged collusion with Russians—he has moved to work with the Russians to defeat ISIS and al-Nusra in Syria. Those are very positive developments and, of course, that is responsive to what President Putin proposed back in September of 2015 at the UN General Assembly, which is a united coalition internationally to fight terrorism, similar to the coalition which emerged to defeat the Nazis during World War II.

Strategic Opportunity

The second area is what he has at least expressed a commitment to, over the course of the campaign and since then. That is to implement Glass-Steagall, which would, as most people know, separate legitimate banking activity involved in investment in real production, real social services, from speculative, casino type banking which has destroyed our economy. He has also, since being elected, made a number of speeches in which he has called for a return to the American System of economy, and has cited Alexander Hamilton, Henry Clay, and Abraham Lincoln among others in that context. And

U.S. Army

U.S. Air Force/Staff Sgt. Lorie Jewell

War presidents: President Bush (top) in Iraq, December 2008; (above) Barack Obama with U.S. Army Gen. David Petraeus, in Iraq.

even in the most recent situation involving Charlottesville, he made the statement that the way to improve human relations, including racial relations in this country, is to create jobs—to actually increase the standard of living of all people in the country, and that involves creating productive jobs, at a higher wage level, so that people can actually afford to have a family and they can afford to make a commitment to a brighter future for the next generation, which is, after all, one of the things that is absolutely critical in anyone's life, is through one's life to contribute to improve conditions for one's children, or if one doesn't have children of one's own, to all children, to posterity. So those are the two areas which are really crucial.

Now with the entire operation to conduct a coup against President Trump, he has not fully acted on those, and in some areas actually acted contrary to that promise. That was the case when he, without evidence that Syria had actually engaged in the use of chemical weapons as claimed, bombed the Syrian air base. The recent speech that he gave on Afghanistan has dangers attached to it, because there is no military solution per se, in Afghanistan, and we've already been there sixteen years with no great results. In fact one thing that has been accomplished in Afghanistan is that the world has been flooded with heroin from the opium crops in that country.

And on the domestic front, there may have been jobs that have been created through the measures that he has taken thus far, including not going along with the free trade agreements, and other similar efforts to bring jobs back to the United States as opposed to outsourcing under these free trade agreements, but the situation has not improved overall. To do that we need to go with Glass-Steagall. We need to go with Lyndon LaRouche's Four Laws, which include Glass-Steagall; which include providing public credit through

Alexander Hamilton

Henry Clay

Abraham Lincoln

a National Bank, with an emphasis on investment in capital-intensive forms of manufacturing, and involve committing ourselves to the future by developing fusion power and by reviving the space program. Those are the things that are necessary right now. Helga and Lyndon LaRouche have called for launching an emergency action in this country to ensure that those policies are actually implemented now, because President Trump is being boxed in. He's certainly combative against his enemies, but he is increasingly being boxed in. You have an environment in the country which the Chinese compare to the Cultural Revolution under Mao Zedong, in terms of the tyranny being set up by the news media and by the former intelligence agents like Clapper, Brennan, Comey, Mueller and his office as Special Counsel—and by Democrats and also opponents of President Trump in the Republican Party. You have a McCarthyite environment that is being created in the country which is extraordinarily dangerous. This is preventing the kind of collaboration which is required with, in particular, the Russians and the Chinese.

Now, we have advocated for a long time that the United States join with the BRICS nations, that is Brazil, Russia, India, China, and South Africa, in terms of what has come to be known as the "One Belt One Road" policy of China, or the Silk Road, or what we used to call the World Land-Bridge, which was initiated by Lyn and Helga LaRouche decades ago, and which the Chinese have adopted. We need to be working with that program, which is a program of peace based on economic development. You see the potential for success by the progress which is being made in Syria now as a result of the fact that the U.S., after President Trump's meeting with President Putin, agreed to setting up a de-escalation zone in southwestern Syria. And now you've got a situation where there may not be direct, joint military action between the United States and Russia against ISIS and al-Nusra, but nonetheless, as the Russian Minister of Defense just said, the civil war in Syria is de-facto over. And now what you have is a very successful effort to wipe out ISIS, not only in Iraq, but also in Syria.

So, that is an example of what can be done. If you take other areas of the world—in North Korea, you could have collaboration between China, Russia, Japan and South Korea to solve that situation, but you would have to agree to do what the Russians and the Chinese have called for—and the Germans have actually advocated this well—which is a dual freeze, where the North Koreans agree no more missile tests, no more nuclear tests, and the United States and South Korea agree no more military drills, which at least in the past, have included the decapitation of the North Korean government. So that's the kind of move you have to take. Similarly in Afghanistan; look at the situation there. Rather than the U.S. going along with NATO militarily after sixteen years of failure, what should be done is collaboration between Russia, China, India, Pakistan, and Iran to settle the crisis in Afghanistan. That's eminently possible to do, but you have to actually make a decision to do that. Similar crises, such as Ukraine, can be solved in the same way.

Development the New Name for Peace

So that represents a New Paradigm of thinking, which is what Helga Zepp LaRouche has referred to. You have the old paradigm, which is based on geopolitics, based on free trade economics, and a certain kind of egoism. And then there is the New Paradigm, which is based upon what the Chinese call a "win-win" approach. This is not just a Chinese invention; this is really the way in which the Thirty Years War in Europe was ended. That was a religious war between Catholics and Protestants that devastated Europe for 30 years. It was ended in the Treaty of Westphalia, in which the principle that defined the peace process, was that you act to the benefit of the other. That's the kind of approach we have to have. That's a win-win strategy.

In a certain sense, what you have, is that most of the rest of the world has adopted the principle of the Treaty of Westphalia, which is having a foreign policy which is based on the advantage of the other, not your narrowly defined self-interest. The rest of the world is committed to a policy of peace and development, which was the policy advocated by the late Pope Paul VI, in an encyclical called *Populorum Progressio,* basically, that the new name of peace is economic development. That's the new paradigm, and if we don't implement that new paradigm now, and fight for that now—which is a global paradigm. It needs to be implemented here in the United States in terms of LaRouche's Four Laws, but it has to be part of a global strategy to be successful. That is what we have to mobilize the American people to understand—that we either do that, or we are facing a danger of the situation spiraling out of control; of complete chaos in the United States, and the removal of a duly elected President from office, for political reasons—by, effectively, a foreign government, the British Empire. And that would mean the danger of thermonuclear war.

That's why Lyndon and Helga LaRouche have said that this is a dire situation requiring emergency action. And so I want to just end with that, and we'll be able to say more in response to your questions.

Speed: Okay, great. Thanks very much, Will. We will be moving to the question portion of this. And while people are thinking of their questions, I think what Will said gives a lot of food for thought, we have to think outside of the box; this is the key thing right now.

We are going to go to the questions that are lined up. Go ahead, can you hear me?

Q 1: This is Sarah from Indiana. And I just wanted to make a comment, but I think what's very important in light of what the gentleman was talking about, is that China has, within 30 years, raised up 700 million people out of poverty in only 30 years. There's a new article floating on the internet that in the last 15 years, the United States has increased terrorism by 6500%; so kind of a little bit of a difference there. The fact that 700 million is over twice the population of the United States. So, it is so vital for people to realize that the United States could be totally out of deficit, if people choose it.

Wertz: Well, I think the other thing to look at is that China, under Mao Zedong and the Cultural Revolution, was a horrendous, tyrannical society in which the population was very much oppressed; particularly intellectuals—people who actually thought—and not just the politically correct views of Chairman Mao and his Little Red Book. Now what you have is a situation where, not only—as you point out—over 700 million people have been lifted out of poverty, but China is playing a very positive role on a global scale, if you look at what they're doing. They're a member of the BRICS, which I mentioned earlier, which is Brazil, Russia, India, China, and the Union of South Africa; a very unique organization because it represents a wide range of countries in the world. They're committed to a policy of economic development. Now the BRICS will have, I think it's its 9th annual summit in China in early September; this will be the 3rd to the 5th of September. The title of the conference is "Stronger Partnership for a Brighter Future." Of course the Chinese have invited the United States to join this effort, which is involved with the "One Belt, One Road"—or the Silk Road— perspective. Obama, of course, refused.

FDR Library

President Franklin D. Roosevelt in Mandan, North Dakota, August 27, 1936.

Obama put massive pressure on other countries, including Japan, Australia, and South Korea, not to work with China in terms of the major development bank which they set up. On the other hand, after his meeting with President Xi, President Trump did send a delegation to the One Belt, One Road summit which occurred in Beijing earlier this year. And this One Belt, One Road effort now includes something like 69 countries; and it's a conception of nations throughout the world working together to lift all of their populations out of poverty, and also to counter the tendency under conditions of poverty for people to be pitted against each other for racial, religious, ethnic, and tribal reasons. Not really good reasons, but to be manipulated against each other under conditions of poverty.

Urgent Changes

So this, in a certain sense, is a model which we should absolutely join at this point; and see it, along with the implementation of LaRouche's Four Laws in the United States, as the means of actually accomplishing rates of growth in the range of 7%-8% per year, as they have achieved in China previously. That's the kind of thing that we have as a potential which we have to move with right now. Again, I stress, this is urgent; it's not something to be done in the distant future. It's urgent because it will also be a tremendous flank on the current effort to unseat the duly-elected President of the United States. If he moves with that, that will mobilize the entire population—the forgotten men and women of this country that he references, as did Franklin Roosevelt. It's the way to actually unite the country, as he said after Charlottesville. It's also something which Rev. Andrew Young, who worked with Martin Luther King, emphasized this past Sunday. He said the biggest problem in the country is poverty, and that that's what you have to focus on, as opposed to turning everything into a race issue.

Speed: OK, very good, and we'll go to the next question. Go ahead.

Q 2: It is the problem that there is such a barrage against the President. The fact that he can function at all is amazing. Outside of our street demonstrations and calling the White House with encouraging words, I don't know what else to do.

Wertz: Really what's required is creativity. And an actual passion for the good, which has traditionally been identified with love for humanity, love for the truth. That which goes to the issue of the Treaty of Westphalia again; that you act to the benefit of others. But the problem is, we've got a situation where the American people have to realize that they also have to think out of the box in terms of how they've been conditioned. I want to give you just one example, which I find very useful. It's the battle of Cannae, which occurred in 216 BC. This was in Italy, and it was fought between the Romans and the Carthaginians. The Carthaginians were led by Hannibal, a Carthaginian general. I'm citing this because it's a good example; it's a classical military example. Of course we're not talking about a military implementation in terms of our action, but we're talking about a state of mind. What he did was, he encircled the Roman troops. The Roman troops amounted to 85,000 total; Hannibal's forces were much less —56,000. They had their backs to a river and the Romans were massing for a frontal assault on Hannibal's forces. What he did was, he created a V-shaped formation, and he drew the Romans into a frontal assault, just marching straight into this V. They actually became entrapped, and they were so densely packed that they couldn't even use their own weapons. Then what he did was, he used his cavalry to encircle the Roman forces and to strike them from the rear. It's an enveloping flanking operation. The Romans were completely devastated; Hannibal lost less than 6000 troops, and the Romans—out of 85,000—lost over 70,000 dead or captured.

What I'm getting at here is an encircling action; I'm getting at getting outside of the box. You've got to actually encircle the enemy from the standpoint of the mind, the standpoint of being creative. That's why there are really two initiatives which we've been engaged in. One is the petition against the intervention in the United States by the British Empire to overthrow a duly-elected U.S. President. Also, to get President Trump to move on the evidence presented by the VIPS—the Veteran Intelligence Professionals for Sanity—that it wasn't Russian hacking; that it was a leak. The whole thing is just a big lie, that's all this is. Just like Adolf Hitler, a big lie; that's what Mr. Binney said.

Q 2 [continued]: If you're going to lie, make it a big one.

The British Factor

Wertz: Right. And even Scott Ritter, the weapons inspector for Iraq, said that having read this report, this borders on sedition against a duly-elected President of the United States. Now, that's one initiative. The second initiative is to move to get President Trump to realize that he has got to encircle the enemy and hit them from the rear. The best way to do that is to go with LaRouche's Four Laws and to join the Silk Road; that's the policy that he needs to move on. So, that's the use of creativity—and you don't get boxed in, you don't operate on the basis of the options which you think you're presented with; which are not good options. They lead to self-destruction. So, you look for the

flanking operation. And these are the two flanking operations which Lyndon and Helga LaRouche have identified.

Q 2 [continued]: That's exactly the point I made when I called the White House. I think I call them two or three times a week. I find that the number I use, instead of the 1111, I call the 1414; that's 202 456-1414. I always get in on that line. They ask me if I want the comment line; I say yes, and I get heard.

Q 3: With the British, this is very good. The main thing that's caused me concern in the last 48 hours is this idea that it's a civil war that we're having, and they're promoting that. I think it's the Trojan Horse. Trump warned us about having a Trojan Horse with these immigrants coming in, and I think that's really what it is. We don't have a civil war, but we have a Soros-funded mercenary army out there fighting with their baseball bats and whatnot. The situation, they upped the ante in the last 24 hours by saying they're bringing in the UN, might come in to protect the Antifa and the Black Lives Matter as a matter of human rights in case we got to having an armed conflict with them, and it looks like they're going to lose. So, that's a potential flare-up that needs to be squelched, and see what kind of British influence is influencing the UN, when we're talking about getting the British influence out. Start squelching them so we don't have that possibility of a UN invasion.

Wertz: I don't think it occurs on that level. The level on which you've got to look at this is how this entire operation against President Trump started. It was started by MI-6, which is the British equivalent of the CIA. A so-called "former" MI-6 agent, Christopher Steele, was paid to put together a dossier of unverified material which he then circulated very widely to Obama's intelligence agency stooges like Brennan and Comey and Clapper. This is the roadmap on which they're operating; so this is straight British intelligence MI-6. The second indication of this is something called the Government Communication Headquarters (GCHQ), which is a pretty dull name for what is the British equivalent of the NSA. They were the ones who, according to the published accounts—and the published accounts may not be completely true, but what the published accounts say is that the head of GCHQ went directly to Brennan. In other words, they don't have to operate under the U.S. Constitution, and the restraints of the U.S. Constitution against surveilling Trump associates, so they surveilled Trump associates all over the world. Then they go to Brennan, the head of the CIA, who's not supposed to operate domestically according to the charter; and he puts together a six-intelligence agency taskforce to begin to investigate Trump in the middle of the Presidential campaign. There are various reports as to when this occurred, some say it was in the Summer of 2016, which is the time of the Republican convention; others say it was before that. But the point is, once Trump was a serious threat to win the nomination, GCHQ began to conduct what would be illegal surveillance in the United States against Trump and his associates. This is all done in collaboration with Obama and with Comey and with Clapper, and with Brennan in particular. And of course, we've gotten from Wikileaks that Brennan put together a cyber warfare unit in the CIA of over 5000 employees; it rivals the NSA.

So, this is what we're talking about. And you see how prominent Clapper and Brennan have been—even in the last few days—in going after President Trump. So the point is, you've got a Clinton-Obama-Comey-Brennan-Clapper operation, which is in fact, funded by Soros. Soros—his pedigree is British; that's what his pedigree is. So, if you go after this and investigate this, then you will upset the entire coup plot. But then combine that—it's got to be combined with the economic program. So, that's the way we have to do it. The other stuff becomes a lower-level fixation which gets you not to think strategically. That's what you've got to do. You've got to clear your mind so you can think strategically and creatively in terms of who the enemy is, and how to defeat the enemy. What we've defined is two initiatives which are critical to defeating the enemy right now; and we've got to get President Trump to move on these as quickly as possible.

Q 3 [continued]: What about Obama giving the internet to the UN?

Solon and Lycurgus

Wertz: Listen, the UN has got all sorts of problems; but frankly, it's not the primary problem in the world. It's basically an assembly of nations; it's as good as it's made. There are good things that are done at the UN when people collaborate. When they don't collaborate, and it's used for geopolitical purposes, including by the British, then it's a mess. For instance, the UN has backed all of the initiatives that have been taken—I mean, look at Syria. You've got Turkey and Iran working together with the Russians. A Sunni country, a predominantly Shi'a country, and they're working with the Russians to defeat terrorism and to restore stability and sovereignty to Syria. That's a positive development which has been backed by the UN Security Council. The UN as a whole in a number of cases has actually positively responded to the Chinese Silk Road, or "One Belt, One Road" Initiative. So, it's really a question of, do the countries who are members of the UN change the way in which they function so they collaborate to solve problems and create a prosperous future for all of mankind? That's the real issue. It has nothing to do with the UN per se as an institution; it's as good or as bad as its members make it. But you have to look beyond the UN, to the question of the British; and you look at it through the whole history. We're talking about two systems, and it goes back before the British.

For instance, the German poet Friedrich Schiller, whom I mentioned earlier, wrote a piece called "On Solon and Lycurgus." Solon was the head of Athens; Lycurgus was the head of Sparta. They had two completely different systems. Solon, as Schiller wrote, had respect for human nature and never sacrificed the people to the state. Never sacrifice the ends to the means; rather he let the state serve the people, and all paths were open to genius. And the basic principle is, the progress of the mind should be the purpose of the state. So, that's like what our country was designed to be; it hasn't always been that, but that's what we would want it to be. That's what you would want other nations to be like. Lycurgus, on the other hand, the way Schiller characterizes him as follows: The laws were iron chains which pulled down the mind. All industry was barred; all science neglected. His state could only persist under one condition—that the mind of the people stagnates. If you look at it, there's another Greek mythology: Zeus was a tyrannical, Olympian so-called "god." He wanted to suppress mankind; he was threatened by the idea that mankind might actually develop technology, develop science, educate themselves, learn languages and so forth. Prometheus gave man fire; that is, technology. He also gave him a Promethean method of thinking, which is the creative method of thinking. So, you have two systems. This means, in a certain sense, that when Helga LaRouche talks about the New Paradigm, she's talking about the paradigm of Solon, the paradigm of Prometheus; versus the imperial policy of depressing

Rodney Dunning

Rodney Dunning

"Left" and "Right" gangs in Charlottesville.

the mental creative capacity of the population in order to maintain political control. The British are like the Roman Empire, like the Venetian Empire; the British Empire has a policy of reducing the world's population and keeping people dumb in order to politically control them.

Q 3 [continued]: Exactly right.

Speed: OK, great. We're going to go on to the next question here. Just say your first name and what state you're calling in from.

Q 4: Hello, this is Wally in Denver. I was reading on the computer about a problem. The Ukrainian government was complaining that Russia was impinging on its sovereignty by constructing a road to Crimea. Do you have any information about that?

From Kiev to Charlottesville

Wertz: Yeah, sure. The picture is straightforward. Obama put Nazis in power in Kiev with the backing of the British and many of the members of the European Union. It's basically part of a strategy to move eastward to the borders of Russia. When the Soviet Union collapsed, it was agreed upon between George H.W. Bush and Gorbachev and other participants, that NATO would not move eastward. But that's precisely what they've done, which is part of a geopolitical strategy. So, they're basically moving to try to encircle Russia, and Ukraine was a critical aspect of that policy. So

what they did was, they backed Nazi groups in Ukraine to take power. Now you had the duly-elected President—Yanukovych—in Ukraine; and under the Constitution of Ukraine, a President cannot be removed from office unless he's impeached. They never impeached him; they never brought impeachment. What they did was use the thugs in the street who were members of what is called the Right Sector, These guys trace themselves back to an actual Nazi who worked with Hitler, named Stepan Bandera. During World War II, his organization was involved in killing tens of thousands of Poles and Jews, working with Hitler. That's what this group traces its background to. The U.S. knows that, because after the war, people like Allen Dulles and MI-6 of Britain brought Bandera and his top aide to London and the United States. Because at that point, they wanted to use the Nazis against the Soviet Union, particularly in Ukraine. The Soviet Union fell, but nonetheless, that's the policy which they've continued to this day. So, they carried out a coup against the duly-elected President, and among the things that they were going to do, is outlaw the use of the Russian language as a second official language in Ukraine. So, the people of Crimea voted in a referendum, called self-determination under the UN Charter, to sever themselves from Ukraine where a coup d'etat had been carried out by Nazis, and to join Russia. So, Russia acknowledged that democratic vote, based on the principle of self-determination in the face of a Nazi coup. Here you've got people in the United States up in arms against Nazi KKK white supremacists; but in fact, Obama put Nazis in power in Ukraine. John McCain backed Nazis in power in Ukraine. The political establishment in Washington DC is backing Nazis in Ukraine; white supremacists in Ukraine. These people who support Nazis then get upset about a staged incident in Charlottesville, which was staged probably with provocateurs both among the Nazis and KKK, and also within the Antifa—the Antifascist organization—the guys with the black masks, black helmets, and black uniforms who carry out violence in all of these events.

So, this thing was set up. If you look at the people involved on the Democratic Party side in Charlottesville, they're all former employees of the State Department, they're all funded by George Soros. As is the mayor, Michael Signer; as is the guy who took the video of the deranged guy who killed one protester and injured others—his name is Brennan Gilmore; and another guy, Tom Periello. They are all funded by, they all worked with John Podesta's Center for American Progress; which is the center of the so-called "Resist" movement against Trump in the United States. And they were all there, along with Virginia Governor Terry McAuliffe, who's a longstanding supporter of the Clintons. They basically immediately used this to go after Trump; it was like you put two chemicals together which you know will react with an explosion. You don't separate the demonstrators, and then you prepare to use the incident—whether you planned the specific incident or not—you use the incident to go after the President of the United States. These are the same guys who backed Nazis in Ukraine. That's the hypocritical irony of this entire operation.

Speed: OK, excellent.

Q 4 [continued]: Then CNN wants to call it civil war, and we're calling that fake news; that it's not civil war.

Not a Civil War

Wertz: Sure. I mean, it's like Syria. It wasn't a civil war. It was a deliberate policy on the part of Obama to carry out regime change against countries which had nothing to do with al-Qaeda. Iraq had nothing to do with al-Qaeda; Libya had nothing to do with al-Qaeda, except to put them in prison. Syria had nothing to do with al-Qaeda. Saudi Arabia did. Britain did. Because

Saudi Arabia is just a satrap of the British Empire. But the point is, that what happened in Syria was that they brought in terrorists from all over the world—from Chechnya in Russia, from Europe, from Tunisia, from Libya, and so forth—in a war of aggression against a sovereign state which is a member of the UN; and then they call it a civil war. But this was Obama; this was one of the great crimes of Obama. This a guy who committed extra-judicial murders against—among others—American citizens after meetings that he held on Tuesdays every week with Brennan in the Oval Office. It would be like Caligula at the Coliseum; he puts his thumb up or down; this guy is to be killed. And that's what they did. So, this is what we're talking about here. The real evil in this thing, is people like Obama. As Lyndon LaRouche has always emphasized, Obama was trained by his stepfather, who was involved in the genocide in Indonesia back in the 1960s; that's where he grew up, with that stepfather. Obama's a murderer and a supporter of Nazis.

Speed: OK, thank you. We have quite a few more questions, so I'm going to move on to the next questioner.

Q 5: This is Greg from St. Louis. Just wanted to make a couple of points for the question out there. One, obviously the analysis of the regime change. The same thing is happening that's attacking the Trump administration, is an attempt to have a regime change, if you will. We simply call it an administration change. So we know all the tools and all the games that they play are related to that. My real issue is the psychosis of Donald Trump himself. I mean, we're putting a lot of marbles in this guy's basket, so to speak. We know he's a wild card; we really didn't know, but for me, it's important that we say what's happening with him as well. It's not like he's not aware of the VIPS report; not like he's not aware of many of these things. My question is, how do we really get him to understand the need to push that VIPS report and get that out there so that we can get at the crux of the Deep State that's attacking him, as well as pushing for this whole war issue, not only within the United States, but across the world?

Wertz: Well, that's—it's not like there's some particular series of tactics that will do this. What we've talked about is two flanks in terms of what he needs to do. In terms of going with the VIPS, going after the

British, and on the other hand, going with LaRouche's Four Laws and the Silk Road. But what you've got to do is, you've got to reach a certain threshold of activity in the country, including among those who support President Trump; but you've also in the process got to create a situation where it becomes much more difficult, as the truth gets out, for certain Democrats and certain Republicans who ran against Trump to carry out the kind of insanity that they're engaged in. So, that's the only way you can do this. You have to mobilize people who support Trump to demand that he take action on these, and that they will support him if he does that. And similarly, you've got to create an environment in which these people like Clapper and Brennan and Comey or Mueller—you've got to box them in. That's why I raised the battle of Cannae in terms of encirclement. The VIPS report boxes in Mueller, it boxes in Comey and Brennan and Clapper. But you've also got to box in the Democrats; these people say they're for Glass-Steagall—many of them. They say they're for working people, some of them; not all that many of them. Certainly Hillary Clinton wasn't too interested in working people. But the point is, that is the party of FDR, the party of Kennedy; or it used to be. So, you've got to really create the situation in which you basically make it clear to them, that if Trump takes the initiative on this, that calls the bluff on these Democrats. They say they're for Glass-Steagall, and yet they're calling for the impeachment of a President who's for Glass-Steagall when Obama was absolutely opposed to Glass-Steagall; as was Hillary Clinton. And they know that.

So, they're engaged in a certain kind of fraud, which needs to be exposed by calling their bluff. If they're real human beings—and you hope that they are on some level—then they'll respond. So you've got to basically do both things by a mobilization of the population.

In the Streets of NY

Q 5 [continued]: How do we box in Trump? I understand boxing in some of those people around him, but Trump himself? His own psychosis is, you're not sure what you're going to get out of this guy at any given time, so you have to force the office of the President to do what you want it to do. So what is that that has to box in Trump, so to speak? I know we've talked about boxing in all these other folks, but he's going to be the head at the head of the arrow; so what are we doing to box him in?

Wertz: We're mobilizing in these two respects; which includes "OK, you said you're for Glass-Steagall. You say that the best way to actually improve human relations, but specifically race relations in this country, is to create jobs." Look at the drug plague. If you don't have decent jobs, which we used to have in urban areas; Baltimore used to have shipbuilding; we used to have steel building, steelworks in Baltimore. Now they've got a tourist harbor, and that's it. You don't have the high-paying jobs that you need, so that people aren't prey to drugs and sales of drugs and so forth, and to gangs—which are related to drugs. So, you've got to actually get him to move on that. But in a certain sense, I think you've just got to convince him that he's combative, but he's not really being combative on the level that he needs to be. He clearly thinks that he is under complete fire; and you can't deny that. They called for his assassination. I put together a list for a webcast last Friday, of the calls for his assassination, impeachment, or forced resignation, or the use of the 25th Amendment against him. This started with the *Spectator*, which is a British paper, saying "Will Donald Trump be assassinated, impeached, or forced to resign?" That was on January 21st. You know the other cases: Johnny Depp, Madonna, Kathy Griffin. You can go through the list. So, you know that this guy really feels that he is under siege. So, he is combative with his tweets and so forth, but the issue here is, if you put this out on the table, if you get this spread widely enough, and he sees that there is support for taking these kinds of actions; and sees that this is an effective flanking operation against those who would destroy this country, then you've got a shot at actually getting him to move on it. That's the only thing I can say.

Speed: Now, that is what we have been doing increasingly in the streets in New York City and in the Midwest and we should expand this. But I'll just give you a sense of some of the results. On Monday, we had three teams out in Manhattan, Staten Island, and Long Island which raised $1400; which is extremely good. We got out about 500 copies of the *Hamiltonian*; we collected a number of petition signatures. What was interesting is that one of these deployments was in the middle of Manhattan, which obviously did not go overwhelmingly for Trump; in fact, it went overwhelmingly for Hillary. So, we were deployed in front of the Fox

Franklin D, Roosevelt signs the Glass-Steagall Act, 1933.

News building in midtown; and pretty much everyone who considered themselves a Trump supporter who came up to our table had already come to the conclusion that Russia-gate and Charlottesville were part of the same operation. We were expecting far more hostility than what existed, and there were several African-Americans who signed on to the petition. Some of them had voted for Trump, some people had not, and so on. And then you got a certain amount of confusion that existed.

We had another deployment, I think this was out in Queens yesterday, where we actually had a gaggle of these women—literally witches; they had everything but the black skirts and broomsticks with them. They came out with signs and so on. It was a very interesting deployment; it was about 10 or 12 of them who rotated through the day, attempting to yell at people, dissuade them from signing up, signing the petition and so on. Their polemic—and this is how you could see it was really organized—it was not around Trump, it was not around Charlottesville; it was actually "Oh, Lyndon La-Rouche. You don't want to sign up with LaRouche; that's a cult. Stop signing up." The response by and large from people coming up was basically, "Get out of my face! I don't want to talk with you; I'm signing up with these people" and so on. So, we ended up, I believe on that deployment, with something like six or seven people getting memberships; lots and lots of people giving their names—over 25 contacts—and so forth and so on.

So, that's what's out there, and I think part of it is that we have to go out and tell the population themselves that they're not doing enough. That's how you box in Trump. We've got to mobilize more of the population; they've got to be organized around a strategic objective. Stop these wars, and go with the economic policy. That's what Trump was voted in for, that's what he's got to do, and that's what the American people have got to demand. That's what was put so beautifully and clearly by Andy Young in his statement on "Meet the Press." Everybody should really read that, and I think that can be very useful in our organizing. So, that's just what I would add to what Will said.

How We Win

Wertz: It's a very principled issue. Countries are destroyed to the extent to which citizens of the countries don't take responsibility for the republic, for their Constitution. That's why the basic concept expressed in the Declaration of Independence is the principle of government by the consent of the governed. Similarly, what Lincoln said—government of, for, and by the people. The basic point is—don't depend on Congress; don't depend on a President. As good as the President may be, they very often are going to operate upon pragmatic conceptions, or what they think is opportune, or what they think is possible for them to do. For instance, the Civil Rights movement had to force it through. They had to force it with Eisenhower, they had to force it with Kennedy, they had to force Johnson to take action. That's the way you have to really look at this. The point is, if you are operating from the standpoint of the vital interests of the nation and of humanity as a whole, you're operating on the basis of principle and of reason; then you have authority within yourself as a citizen of a country—and also the responsibility as a citizen of a country, and as a citizen of the world—to take action and see that those actions which are required are acted upon by an elected official. They're supposed to represent us; they get elected by us, and they're supposed to represent our best interests. I think that's really the issue. And you have to educate yourself so that you

know for certain with scientific certainty, that what you're advocating is actually a policy which is required and must be implemented.

What we've defined, is a policy that must be implemented. Take the Four Laws. You have Democrats who say they're for Glass-Steagall, but they're brainwashed in terms of Green ideology. The rest of the Four Laws that Lyndon LaRouche has put forward, put an emphasis on capital intensive forms of investment, including nuclear energy, nuclear desalination, the development of fusion, the expansion of the space program. Many of these Democrats say they're for Glass-Steagall, but what do they mean by Glass-Steagall if they're Green? Then on the Republican side, many of them are not Greenies, in the sense of being opposed to technological progress, but they've been brainwashed in respect to a balanced budget or merely reducing a deficit. So, they have no conception of the idea of public credit, and no conception of what Hamilton put forward with a National Bank, or what Lincoln put forward with greenbacks, or what Franklin Roosevelt put forward with the bank that he used to actually engage in investment in the economy—it was the Reconstruction Finance Corporation. After the war in Germany, they had the Kreditanstalt für Wiederaufbau, which is the Credit Institution for Reconstruction; same principle. But the idea is that the government can extend credit as a sovereign nation, can extend credit for productive investment. The problem here is that many Republicans have no conception of that.

So, you've got to educate both Democrats and Republicans to understand a scientific conception of economics; which they don't have. It's not clear exactly whether Trump has it; he may reference Hamilton and Henry Clay, and Abraham Lincoln, but it's not clear from his actions so far that he has those conceptions. So, it's a question of educating, it's a question of mobilizing your fellow citizens to ensure that the policies the nation needs—the world needs—are enacted. It's a very basic principle that the power of government to govern derives from the people; but it has to be an educated people, not a mob.

Speed: OK, great. Will, we have about five more minutes, but we have about six more questions. So, we're going to try to get to as many of them as possible. I want to ask everybody to keep your questions and comments at this point short and succinct so we can try to get through as many of these as we can. OK, go ahead.

How the British Subverted Us

Q 6: Yeah, this is Ken in Moline, Illinois. Is the CIA a subsidiary of MI-6?

Wertz: You have to go back to World War II and the aftermath of World War II. The British Empire backed Hitler, and they wanted him to go east against the Soviet Union; but Hitler at a certain point decided that he was going to go west. Churchill knew he couldn't defeat Hitler on the continent, so he needed to bring the U.S. into the war. Roosevelt certainly wanted to defeat fascism, but the British actually set up covert operations of British intelligence, MI-6, MI-5, in the United States at Rockefeller Center. They worked closely with Allen Dulles who became Deputy CIA Director and then later CIA Director after Roosevelt died. So, the point is, in 1946 there was an agreement signed which was called the UK-U.S.A. Agreement. Then later it became what's called the Five Eyes, which is Australia, New Zealand, Canada, Britain, and the United States. Basically the problem here is that our intelligence agencies here in the United States are working directly with British intelligence and with other members of the British Empire, or what's called now the Commonwealth.

There may be patriots within these intelligence agencies, many of them have become whistleblowers. But yet, this is how the British have subverted U.S. intelligence.

Speed: OK, very good. We're going to take two more questions now; and in about three minutes or maybe we'll go a little bit over. Go ahead.

Q 7: This is Steve from Pennsylvania. What I've noticed with the different organizations I've worked with—I work with several different patriot organizations, including the Oath Keepers and the Three Percenters and some militia that were there in Charlottesville the day of that event. From my different sources, I understand that these groups on both sides were all hooked in with State Department and Obama appointees and employees and Occupy Wall Street and those groups. Could Charlottesville be considered like a false flag to try to push this narrative of this race card thing, since the Russia thing completely failed and they now want to push the 25th Amendment thing and they want to push that Trump somehow has dementia?

Wertz: You're right; it's a false flag operation. For instance, one of the things that came out is that one of the organizers of the demonstrators—a guy named Kessler—I think it was Charles Grassley who asked the question, or another Senator—this guy was involved in Occupy Wall Street. He was apparently a supporter of Obama. Then all of a sudden, you're expected to believe that there was this transformation, and he ends up being an organizer of this demonstration. So that's on the one side. On the other side, as I said at the beginning—I don't know if you heard it or not—all of the key players in Charlottesville are Democrats who have worked with John Podesta at the Center for American Progress; which described itself as the institutional center of the Resist movement against Trump in the United States. And Podesta, of course, is Obama, he's Clinton—both Hillary and Bill. This is all funded by Soros. So, the whole thing was in that sense, a set-up. And it's modelled upon what they did in Ukraine; where it was the State Department, it was Soros, and so forth. Think about how that thing operated. For instance, when Yanukovych was forced to flee, he was accused of ordering snipers to shoot demonstrators. But he denies that that was the case, and there's evidence that the snipers may have actually been members of the Right Sector, the Nazis; or organized by them. So, it is a false flag operation. This whole operation was set to take off after Charlottesville. Remember, Charlottesville was declared by the mayor of Charlottesville, Signer, as a capital of the Resistance in a speech he gave on January 31st earlier this year. The point is, Charlottesville was designed as a center of the resistance to Trump before this incident occurred.

Wertz: [After intervening questions.] I just want to go back to the remarks that you cited from Lyndon LaRouche at the very beginning, Lynne, to underscore the urgency of the situation. Again, what he said is that we have to win now; if we lose, we are finished because we will be destroyed by the people opposed to what he is doing in terms of the initiatives we're taking. The existence of the United States depends upon doing the job. It's not making suggestions; it's getting victory against the causes of the things that are destroying the ability of the United States to express itself properly.

So, I just wanted to end with that. I thought the questions tonight were very responsive and showed that people have a sense of the urgency of this. So, our job is to organize a lot of other people. I encourage people to do that, and figure out creative ways in which they can do that. Like the lady who just spoke, get in touch with us in terms of what you might be able to do with us or with others in our movement who may be in your vicinity.

Speed: OK; excellent. So, that concludes the LaRouche activist call for Thursday. We'll be talking with all of you very soon. Hopefully, with lots more results on the petitioning and other activities. Good night.

Poe's Poet-Mathematician: Evariste Galois

by David Shavin

Poe's Dupin: "As poet and mathematician, he would reason well; as mere mathematician, he could not have reasoned at all."

Poe's Narrator to Dupin: "You have a quarrel on hand, I see," said I, "with some of the algebraists of Paris ..."

Charles Dupin (1819) on Descriptive Geometry

On the "general and purely rational geometry, of which descriptive geometry is only the graphic translation ... one's mind must be especially trained in this general geometry. One must be able to represent the shapes of bodies in space, and to ideally combine these shapes by the sole power of imagination. The mind learns to see inwardly and with perfect clarity the individual lines and surfaces, and families of lines and surfaces; it acquires a feeling for the character of these families and individuals; it learns to see them, combine them, and foresee the results of their intersections and of their more or less intimate contacts, etc. Thus the new geometry greatly strengthens the imagination; it teaches you how to grasp a vast collection of shapes quickly and precisely, to judge their similarities and differences and their relations of size and position ..." For example, regarding designing roads or railways through the countryside, "... engineering drawings are needed only for limited areas in which the best route to follow is easily

Evariste Galois

determined from the overall direction discovered by the geometric overview. It was this grand manner of considering the shapes of nature, which was discovered by the students of Monge ..."[1]

I. Dupin, Poe's Poet-Mathematician

Aug. 20—In 1841, Edgar Allan Poe created the fictional character, the poet mathematician C. Auguste Dupin. He first appears in "The Murders in the Rue Morgue" (MRM), in which his "descriptive geometry" method succeeds in solving the crime, while the detailed and exhaustive methods of Police Prefect G____ prove hopeless. In the previous year, 1840, Prefect G____, that is, the Police Prefect of Paris, Henri Louis Gisquet, had issued his *Memoires*, which included a curious dismissal of the violent death of Evariste Galois, one of the poet-mathematician students of Gauss' epic, *Disquisitiones Arithmeticae*.[2] The case is made here that Poe's poet-mathematician, in real life, was Galois, and further, that Poe's Dupin would secure justice for Galois.

---

1. Charles Dupin, 1819, "Historical Essay on the Contributions and Scientific Works of Gaspard Monge," translated by Larry Hecht.
2. "The Generation of 'Poet-Mathematicians': The Case of Niels Abel," by David Shavin, *EIR*, Vol. 44, Issue 30, July 28, 2017.

First, we look at Poe's characterization of the particular genius of Dupin. In MRM, the first of Poe's three "Dupin" tales, Poe challenges the reader with his Narrator's (N's) description of Dupin's unique method of analysis. After walking together in silence for a quarter-hour, Dupin casually reads N's mind with a line that seems to come from nowhere—that the actor Chantilly is indeed too short for the role of "Xerxes." N is dumbstruck. By what power had Dupin divined N's private thoughts?

Dupin explains his chain of reasoning: A stranger had bumped N, causing a brush with a pile of paving stones and discomfort to his ankle. A bit later on, upon encountering some advanced street paving, with "overlapping and riveted blocks," Dupin noticed that N's face brightened, and N murmured the word, "stereotomy." (So, the art of three-dimensional cutting and fashioning—an element of descriptive geometry—can improve life, helping to avoid injuries from more backward alleyways.) The two of them had shared discussions on stereotomy, so the matter of the properties of constituent parts being developed from the characteristics of the larger dimensionality was a shared thought process. From their recent discussions about both Epicurus and "atomies," or how the properties of the very small come about, the next part of their recent discussions was suggested.

This was, how the ancient Epicurus' conjectures were in line with recent astronomical developments, that of the nebular cosmogony and the nebula of Orion! (Poe refers to a Dr. Nichol, a popularizer of John Herschel's work on the organization, beyond the solar system, of galaxies.)[3] When N next turned to look up at the stars, Dupin felt confirmed in his reasonings. Dupin reminded N that they had both read and discussed, in the previous day's newspaper, a reference to Orion, which was included as part of an attack upon the actor Chantilly. When N smiled and altered his "stooping" posture, drawing himself up to full height, Dupin knew that N made the connection from Orion to the diminutive Chantilly playing roles that were too big for him.

illustration by Frédéric Théodore Lix

C. Auguste Dupin, illustration for The Puloined Letter *by Edgar Allan Poe.*

Only then had Dupin dared to articulate: "He is a very little fellow, that's true, and would do better for the Theatres des Varietes."

What should one make of a power to trace causal moves of the imagination and of the mind, combined with a few selected empirical confirmations? Before dismissing Dupin's bold reasoning, consider N's reflection: "There are few persons who have not, at some period of their lives, amused themselves in retracing the steps by which particular conclusions of their own minds have been attained. The occupation is often full of interest; and he who attempts it for the first time is astonished by the apparently illimitable goal." Is there any child whose imagination has led him or her, perhaps at night before falling asleep, down strange avenues—and who, occasionally, hasn't asked himself how he arrived at that point in his internal dialogue? There is a marvelous power to be acquired, though with no little difficulty, in training oneself, after allowing the imagination to roam, to then retrace the steps, working backwards. One learns secrets about oneself and, also, one develops the power of mind, of analysis. Poe's boldness is that he openly, audaciously, addresses the development of that power.

In 1842, Poe's Dupin character reappears in "The Mystery of Marie Roget," based upon an actual, unsolved murder case in New York City. Dupin is further

---

3. Dr. J.P. Nichol's 1838 *Views of the Architecture of the Heavens* featured an engraved plate from Herschel's telescope, both shocking and charming the public with a representation of our Milky Way galaxy.

developed in "The Purloined Letter" (1844). There, a crafty minister in the French government has stolen a document that compromises the Queen, and proceeds to blackmail her over policy matters. The minister is waylaid and searched more than once by Gisquet's minions, to rule out his carrying the document on his person. It is known that the document is in the minister's apartments, a finite area that Gisquet has searched inch by inch in excruciating detail. Dupin tells Gisquet that the minister "… is not altogether a fool, and, if not, must have anticipated these waylayings, as a matter of course." "Not altogether a fool," said Gisquet, "but then he's a poet, which I take to be only one remove from a fool." "True," said Dupin, "… although I have been guilty of certain doggerel myself." Dupin proceeds to discover the document almost immediately, astonishing N; and he does so, based primarily upon his analysis of the minister's mind. He explains Gisquet's shortcoming:

"This functionary, however, has been thoroughly mystified; and the remote source of his defeat lies in the supposition that the Minister is a fool, because he has acquired renown as a poet. All fools are poets; this the Prefect feels, and he is merely guilty … in thence inferring that all poets are fools."

"But is this really the poet?" I asked. "There are two brothers, I know; and both have attained reputation in letters. The Minister I believe has written learnedly on the Differential Calculus. He is a mathematician, and no poet."

"You are mistaken; I know him well; he is both. As poet and mathematician, he would reason well; as mere mathematician, he could not have reasoned at all, and thus would have been at the mercy of the Prefect."

"You surprise me," I said, "by these opinions, which have been contradicted by the voice of the world. You do not mean to set at naught the well-digested idea of centuries. The mathematical reason has long been regarded as the reason par excellence."

"… The mathematicians, I grant you, have done their best to promulgate the popular error to which you allude, and which is none the less an error for its promulgation as truth … [Further, T]hey have insinuated the term 'analysis' into application to algebra. The French are the originators of this particular deception…."

"You have a quarrel on hand, I see," said I, "with some of the algebraists of Paris …"

"The great error lies in supposing that even the truths of what is called pure algebra, are abstract or general truths."

Poe and Galois

Compare Poe and Galois. Poe's 1844: "… The mathematicians, I grant you, have done their best to promulgate the popular error to which you allude, and which is none the less an error for its promulgation as truth … [Further, T]hey have insinuated the term 'analysis' into application to algebra. The French are the originators of this particular deception…." In January 1831, the revolutionary 19-year-old, Galois, gave a series of classes in a Paris bookstore for the youth of Paris. His introduction: "Of all human knowledge, we know that mathematics is the most abstract, the most logical, the only one which does not appeal to the world of our sense impressions. Often one concludes that mathematics is, on the whole, the most methodic, the most coordinated branch of science. But this is an error.

"Take any book on algebra, whether a textbook or an original work, and you will see in it a confused mass of propositions, whose rigor contrasts strangely with the disorder of the whole structure. It would seem that the ideas are so precious to the author that he abhors the pain of connecting them with each other, while at the same time his mind is so exhausted by the concepts which form the foundations of his work that he cannot produce one single thought that would coordinate this ensemble. Sometimes you seem to encounter a method, a connection, a coordination. But all this is wrong and artificial. You will find divisions of material for which there is no reason, arbitrary connections, conventional arrangements. These faults, still more glaring than the absence of all method, you will find chiefly in books written by men who do not know what they are writing about. All this must seem especially astonishing to people for whom the word 'mathematics' is synonymous with 'rigor.' "

This is Infeld's translation of Galois' notes. It seems to be his reconstruction of the opening of the lecture series. He notes: "The lecture given in Caillot's bookshop is genuine Galois; it is based on one of Galois' notes in his posthumous papers."

II. A Quarrel with the Algebraists of Paris

Evariste Galois was the genius who, more than anyone else of the time, developed Gauss' approach to the underlying laws of "pure algebra." Galois' method revived the physical geometry approach of the five Platonic solids and of Kepler, as transmitted through Gauss.[4] Of this, more below. It was the chief algebraist of Paris, Augustin-Louis Cauchy, who did all he could to bury Galois' manuscript. It was Cauchy's factional allies who did all they could to bury Galois. Poe, a decade later, found the matter worth reviving.

Now for a brief introduction of two leading characters. Cauchy was a loyal administrator for the Restoration monarchs, Louis XVIII and Charles X, imposed upon France, 1815 to 1830, in the wake of the Congress of Vienna. In 1815, Gaspard Monge and Lazare Carnot were thrown out of their republican Ecole Polytechnique, and Cauchy was installed as overseer. In two infamous and thuggish cases, Cauchy accepted scientific treatises, under the obligation of making a report on them to the Academy of Sciences, and instead, he buried them. In 1826, Cauchy had buried Niels Abel's scientific treatise and, despite the hazard of a second such extraordinary "accident," he was not embarrassed to repeat this performance in 1829 with Galois' first two submissions—and very likely, even Galois' third submission in 1830. (Four unlikely accidents occurring one after the other—but if anyone could calculate the odds of that occurring, Cauchy could!) When Charles X abdicated in July 1830, Cauchy left France, leaving his family behind. He would spend five years trying to tutor an unwilling teenager, the grandson of Charles X and his chosen heir to the throne, as part of their plan to reconquer France.

Henri-Joseph Gisquet, Police Prefect in Paris from 1831 to 1836, was likely the man most responsible for the death, at age 20, of Evariste Galois. He certainly led the suppression of Galois' political movement. Poe's MRM tale identifies Gisquet's methods with those of an earlier prefect, Vidocq, and Poe would have been familiar with at least parts of both of their memoirs.[5] Gisquet's own memoir, published in 1840, the year prior to the appearance of C. Auguste Dupin, included the type of attempted coverup of Galois' death that Poe would have recognized immediately. It made for a case worthy of Dupin's analytic abilities. Poe concludes his "Murders in the Rue Morgue" with Dupin's skewering of Police Prefect Gisquet: "I like him especially for one master stroke of cant, by which he has attained his reputation for ingenuity. I mean the way he has 'of denying what is, and explaining what isn't.'" Gisquet's explanation of Galois' death: A friend killed him.

III. 'What Is'—The Genius of Galois

Both Cauchy and Gisquet did their best to deny what is—that Galois was a genius. First, a quick characterization of Galois' approach.

Galois had just turned fifteen, in the Paris of 1826, when Abel's method for analyzing higher-powered equations was announced to the French Academy. Between 1823 and 1829, Dirichlet, Abel, and then Galois—all based on Gauss' work—had treated the curious situation in which equations up to the fourth power could be submitted to algorithms, but beginning with the fifth power, the "quintic," nature seemed to defy such treatment. Even though Cauchy had buried Abel's paper (and Abel had died a month or two before Galois' first two papers were presented to the French Academy), Galois had effectively succeeded in extending Abel's approach to the quintic, and to solving higher-powered equations in general. In so doing, he developed a higher-powered language to examine what was going on. Imagine Cauchy's frustration in June 1829, when he realized his earlier, thuggish action might be to no avail.

Galois developed an analysis of equations based upon the symmetries, and non-symmetries, of the five Platonic solids. An equation could be factored, could be broken into constituent parts, if symmetries, or even partial symmetries, could be located. If no symmetries were locatable, the equation could not be factored. (These symmetries are typically explained by delving into the symmetries in the representation of the coefficients, or characteristics of a formula, by matrices. However, the fascination with bookkeeping matters there, tends to obscure the principle.) A simple case of this type of analysis is reflected in the exercise students go through in determining whether a number is composite or prime—the factors are primitive "subgroups" of a number.

---

4. For example, compare the bulk of Gauss's 1799 "Fundamental Theorem of Algebra" with his drawing at the end.
5. Portions of Vidocq's memoirs appeared in *Burton's Magazine*, 1838-1839. Poe was an editor of *Burton's* in 1839-1840.

A somewhat more complicated case arises with Gauss' analysis, where some bases revolve through a given modulus without ever repeating until all possible residues are given, while others form subgroups of repeated patterns before they ever cover all the possible residues. The powers of three—3, 9, 27, 81, etc.—are expressed in a modulus-5 system as 3, 4, 2, 1. (These are what is "left over," the residue, after the modulus of five is divided into the number.) These four "residues" will keep repeating, and they cover all the possibilities in a modulus-5 world. However, the powers of four—4, 16, 64, 256, etc.—become 4, 1, 4, 1, etc. Four, in modulus-5, forms a subgroup that does not exhaust all the possibilities. In the modulus-5 world, 3 acts, loosely speaking, more "prime"-like than the more "composite"-like 4.

The power of mind had to be developed to "see" the rich interplay amongst the five Platonic solids (the cube, tetrahedron, octahedron, icosahedron, and "first among equals," the dodecahedron—whence the other four are best situated).[6] Galois developed that new language, involving what are called modular functions. When confronted with an apparent barrier at the fifth power, Galois took Abel's hint that we would not solve—and properly benefit from—this barrier by any normal extension of the methods developed from 2nd, 3rd, and 4th power solutions. And he took the Creator's hint, just as in Plato's *Timaeus* dialogue, that man is fulfilling his historical mission if he pursues the mysterious and rather miraculous, unseen powers that are

---

6. Unfortunately, the closest most students get to even a hint of such symmetries is in the expansion of a sum raised to a power. They are told to use Pascal's Triangle, in which the same coefficient appears symmetrically. (That is, for a fifth power expansion, having six terms, they pair up as 1st and 6th, the 2nd and 5th, and the 3rd and 4th.) However, even this simple symmetrical character is left unaddressed and unexplained. Instead, the student gets the practical advice: "Learn the rule. It works."

From Galois to 'Group Theory'

Felix Klein, in his *Lectures on the Icosahedrons and the Solution of Equations of the Fifth Degree,* would give permission to mathematicians to neutralize the Platonic solids, treating them as merely a representation equivalent to the matrices. But there is a difference between the foot and the footprint. As a result, Galois' employment of the word *groupe* has become the label for a group theory in which most "group theoreticians" end up playing with the numbers with little or no idea of the "descriptive geometry" approach rooted in the Platonic solids. (A related, but simpler, illustration of this is involved in the preference for digital computation over analogue computers.) Klein's problem originated in the mistake that we had Poe's Dupin cite earlier, "they have insinuated the term 'analysis' into application to algebra. The French are the originators of this particular deception...."

Leibniz's "analysis situs" is neutered and assimilated into previous algebraic techniques. See Lyndon LaRouche, in his "How Bertrand Russell Became an Evil Man" (*Fidelio*, Fall 1984), who identified the Klein problem as such: "Those choices of starting points set the stage for Klein's crucial, false assumption, set forth on pp. 58-59 [of Klein's *Famous Problems*]: 'The period from 1670 to 1770, characterized by the names of Leibniz, Newton, and Euler, saw the rise of modern analysis. Great discoveries followed one another in such an almost unbroken series that, as was natural, critical rigor fell into the background. For our purposes the development of the theory of series is especially important.' With that silly bit of pedagogical hand waving there, you have Klein's hoax set into place on stage. Henceforth, everything said by Klein is an extension of that whopper, that fallacy of composition.

"The crucial code words from that citation are 'analysis' and infinite 'series'. Those code words' appearance rightly implies that Klein is not addressing the ontological problem of species distinction, which he only pretends to be attacking; he is engaged in a sleight of hand, pretending to address an ontological problem, while considering only a formal one. He is addressing a problem in infinite series; he is using the credibility of Hermite's and Lindemann's work on this problem of infinite series, to deflect the viewer's attention from the fact that he is not addressing the ontological problem at all. That is the formal nature of his fraud."

found to shape and structure the world as presented to us.

Again, Charles Dupin's discussion of "descriptive geometry," ten years prior to Galois' paper, appears as an excellent estimate of Galois' process: "One must be able to represent the shapes of bodies in space, and to ideally combine these shapes by the sole power of imagination. The mind learns to see inwardly and with perfect clarity the individual lines and surfaces, and families of lines and surfaces; it acquires a feeling for the character of these families and individuals; it learns to see them combine them, and foresee the results of their intersections and of their more or less intimate contacts, etc. Thus the new geometry greatly strengthens the imagination; it teaches you how to grasp a vast collection of shapes quickly and precisely, to judge their similarities and differences and their relations of size and position...."

IV. Galois, Revolutionary-Mathematician

Poe has the Narrator in "The Purloined Letter" address Dupin: " 'You have a quarrel on hand, I see,' said I, 'with some of the algebraists of Paris ...' " Galois was the outstanding example of Dupin's quarrel with the algebraists of Paris. We wish to deal with Galois' last year, before his death at age 20, as a prisoner of Police Prefect Gisquet. For that purpose, let's fill in Galois' story with a summary of his tumultuous last three years, beginning with his first submission to the French Academy of Sciences.

Cauchy Buries Galois' Paper

Galois, still five months shy of eighteen, submitted two papers to the Academy of Sciences on May 25 and June 1, 1829. Cauchy took possession of them, as he was to make the report on them to the Academy. Then on June 22, 1829, the news of the April 7 death of Niels Abel was announced at the French Academy. At the time, Cauchy had held Abel's *memoire* for three years, and Galois' for only three weeks. Karl Jacobi, the collaborator of both Abel and Lejeune Dirichlet, brought attention to Cauchy's malfeasance, and attempted to get Abel's manuscript from Cauchy. There was evident ner-

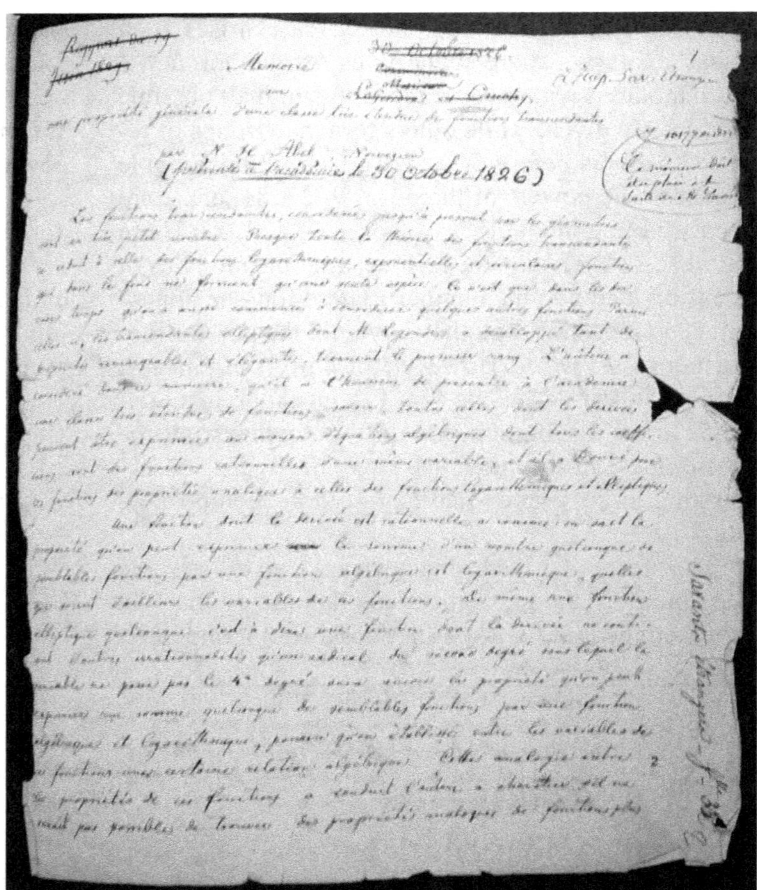

Niels Abel's manuscript that was buried by Cauchy.

vousness at the Academy over Cauchy's heavy-handed tactics, for Legendre seems to have manufactured a cover story for Cauchy. He pretended to Jacobi that he and Cauchy had agreed to ask Abel for a neater copy, since "we perceived that the memoir was barely legible; it was written in ink almost white, the letters badly formed ..." However, when the document was finally dug out of the Academy in 1840, it was quite legible—remaining so even today.[7] Clearly, something was clouding the "perceptions" in Paris, and there is no reason to believe Abel was at fault for failing to provide a "neater copy." Jacobi's 1829 inquiry, in bringing attention to Cauchy's previous fraud, would normally have been enough for most ideologues to give pause before claiming a second misplacing of a submitted paper.[8]

----

7. Legendre's evasion suggests that he estimated Cauchy's intent, as of the Spring of 1829, that the document would never see the light of day. Otherwise, he likely would not have ventured such a cover.

8. Abel's manuscript was not produced until 1840, upon official diplomatic pressure of the Norwegian consul.

At this same time that Galois was launching his scientific career, his father died under bizarre circumstances. Nicholas-Gabriel Galois, the popular and witty mayor of a small town near Paris for the previous fifteen years, was targeted for destruction by the town's new Jesuit priest, who had allied himself with some Ultramontanists, local enemies of the mayor. They manufactured a scandal by circulating vulgar epigrams directed against locals, and forging the mayor's name to them. On July 2, 1829, Nicholas-Gabriel was found dead, asphyxiated in an apart-

painting by Pierre-Narcisse Guérin

Charles X

painting by Franz Xaver Winterhalter

Louis-Philippe

ment in Paris. A note was left for Galois from his father, explaining that the ugliness left him no choice.

In January 1830, Cauchy finally did agree to report to the Academy on Galois' historic paper. However, Cauchy wrote, on January 18, that he was not well, and that he had to delay his report until the next week. The following week Cauchy did show up; however, he made a presentation on his own work, never mentioning Galois or his manuscript. What happened that week to Cauchy, certainly, would make for a curious story; but what is one to think of the other scientists at the Academy, staring at the naked emperor of the Hans Christian Andersen story?

After that performance, it had to be pretty clear that Galois might not be getting his two manuscripts back any time soon. In February 1830, Galois rewrote his two papers into one submission for the Grand Prize in Mathematics contest. That new paper went to the Academy's permanent secretary, Joseph Fourier. We may presume that Cauchy got the paper from Fourier, since Galois evidently reported, to his close friend, Auguste Chevalier, that Cauchy had seen this new paper. However, that paper also was lost, and consequently was eliminated from the Grand Prize determination.[9] That

spring, Galois turned to the *Bulletin de Ferussac* to publish three new short items. Ferussac and his group were the ones who had aided and employed Abel in 1826.[10]

Revolutionary Activities

It was at this point, July 9, 1830, that King Charles X announced that he would solve his problems over the growing electoral success of his opposition. He would simply rule by ordinance. His repressive ordinances on July 25, 1830 were the immediate trigger for the July Revolution, whereby the republicans around Lafayette settled for an arrangement with Louis-Philippe, making him the "Citizen-King." Charles X abdicated in favor of his ten-year-old grandson and left for London. Galois joined Lafayette's National Guard—notably, the Artillery Unit section, the core of the republicans.

That same Fall, a fellow member of the Artillery Unit, the scientist François-Vincent Raspail, recruited

---

Fourier died in May 1830 and the Galois paper was not found among the other papers in Fourier's study. This is rather transparent, as no other submitted papers were similarly lost.

10. Shavin, see note 2. In 1831, the government would cancel the subscriptions of its various bureaus to Ferussac's journal, causing financial hardship and loss of control over the journal. The journal died shortly thereafter, following the Republic to the grave.

---

9. Blame for the lost paper is somehow associated with the fact that

Galois to his more militant republicans of the Society of Friends of the People.[11] In December, Louis-Philippe ordered the disbanding of the Artillery Unit, the dismissal of Lafayette as head of the National Guard, and the arrest of nineteen of its leaders. They were suspected of planning to turn over their heavy artillery to "the people" and are charged with a conspiracy to overthrow the government. They were tried in April 1831.

On March 13, 1831, financier Casimir Périer replaced Pierre Laffitte as both President of the Council of Ministers and Finance Minister. Typical of the machinations now afoot, the government offered to confer membership in the Legion of Honor on Raspail, a noted scientist in his own right. He viewed

Gilbert du Motier, Marquis de Lafayette

painting by Joseph-Désiré Court

it as the bribe that it was, and signed his refusal "Raspail, plain citizen." Périer made clear the government's game involving Raspail: "He must accept or else rot in a dungeon!"[12] The government's actions from December 1831 to April 1832—involving the dismissal of Lafayette, the dismantling of the Artillery Unit of the National Guard, the arrests of the Nineteen, the dumping of Laffitte for Périer—made it clear that the "Citizen-King" was more the "Financier's-King."

On April 16, 1831, all nineteen republican leaders were found innocent, with great public celebration. Then on May 10, 1831, Galois was arrested for his role, the previous evening, at a dinner party for the Nineteen. Of his last twelve months of life, Galois would spend ten of them imprisoned, most of them at Sainte-Pélagie prison.

---

11. Raspail identified the goals of the "Friends of the People" in his January 1832 court case: "… an elected executive with a short term in office; a constitution, … universal military service without replacement; juries chosen by lot from among all citizens; freedom of the press, assembly , and worship; the right to work; and the abolition of the death penalty." See Dora B. Weiner's *Raspail: Scientist and Reformer*, p. 171.
12. Laffitte, much more the industrial banker, had been undermined by Périer throughout the first seven months of Louis-Philippe's administration. (Laffitte is named by Dumas as the source of Poe's funds in Paris in 1832.)

What had Galois done at the famous May 9 celebration dinner, attended by two hundred or so republican enthusiasts, many of them dressed in their National Guard uniforms? After the official (pre-arranged) toasts ended, more spontaneous toasts ensued. Etienne Arago, for example, received an enthusiastic response to his: "I drink to the Sun of 1831. May it be as warm as that of 1830, but not blind us as the other did!"

Amidst these sentiments, Galois put a point on matters. With one hand holding his wine glass and the other his meat knife, he calls out, "To Louis-Philippe!" A ruckus ensued. Then he continues with words not well heard over the hubbub, "… if he betrays his oaths." Alexandre Dumas, in attendance, reported that, because of the presence of police agents, he "didn't care to be compromised" and he "jumped from the window sill into the garden." That night, the police agents at the dinner did indeed report Galois, and the next day he was arrested at his home and taken to prison.

Prison and Auguste Chevalier

At his trial, on June 15, the judge probed Galois as to why he was afraid the King would betray France. Galois was, typically, simple and direct: "Everything encourages us to adopt this position … it is reasonable to believe that Louis-Philippe could betray the Nation. He has not given us enough guarantees … [A]ll the King's actions, though not yet showing his bad faith, can lead us to doubt his good faith. One example is the background of intrigue to his accession to the throne." At that point, he was prevented from going further, but it is a good bet that Périer's name was about to enter the analysis. Galois' lawyer suggested to the judge that this line of questioning may get into matters better left alone, to which the prosecution quickly agreed.

Galois concluded, not as simply this time: "I confess my behavior [with the toast] was rather sly. You can surely imagine the police inspector's joy, when he thought he had unmasked a conspirator … [However,] I cannot let what the public prosecutor said, about it being impossible for the King to be a traitor, go unanswered. Nobody is foolish enough to believe now that a king is perfect, especially since when judges—who under Charles X, persecuted us, because we said that the King could neglect his duties—have themselves now sworn allegiance to another man, who had been placed on the throne, as the result of his predecessor's stupid behavior." In one extended sentence, he managed to circumvent his lawyer, the prosecutor and the judge. The jury ruled that Galois was not guilty.

On the day of Galois' trial, his loyal friend, Auguste Chevalier, published in *Le Globe* both praise of Galois' mathematical genius and condemnation of the unfair treatment directed toward him. It related the story of the third lost paper, the one submitted for the Grand Prize sixteen months earlier. Galois added that in January 1831, he had rewritten that memoire and resubmitted it, but that Poisson at the Academy had sat on it. Three weeks after Chevalier's publication, on July 4, 1831, Poisson reported to the Academy that Galois' paper was, as far as they understood, not worthy and was to be returned to Galois.

Galois was arrested for the second and last time on Bastille Day, July 14, 1831. This was to be the first Bastille Day since the July Revolution of 1830, and the police moved pre-emptively. During the night of July 13/14, Republican leaders were arrested in their homes; but Galois, perhaps as a precaution, was not at home. On the 14th, in uniform, he led a group of 600 demonstrators. The police were waiting for Galois at a bridge, and he was arrested and jailed with, again, no violence from the demonstrators. He was put back into the Sainte-Pélagie prison. There he joined his colleague, Raspail, who had been arrested and convicted the day after the May 9 celebration dinner. Evidently, Galois was jailed for three more months before he was finally charged—and the charge would be for bearing arms and wearing the uniform of the disbanded Artillery Unit

François-Vincent Raspail

of the National Guard.

Some time in October, during those three months of uncharged detention, Galois was shown the rejection letter from the Academy of Sciences, informing him that Poisson could not understand Galois' paper. (At least Galois' fourth submission was not "misplaced" as were the previous three—perhaps one of the few accomplishments of the glorious events of 1830, the July Revolution and the flight of Cauchy!) Galois turned to Auguste Chevalier to privately publish his material. It was in one of these letters from prison that December that Galois tells Auguste: "I must tell you how manuscripts go astray in the portfolios of the members of the Institute, although I cannot in truth conceive of such carelessness on the part of those who already have the death of Abel on their consciences." It also raises the question, what could Auguste conceive when his correspondent was dead within six months?

V. Gisquet vs. the 'Fierce Republican'

Why Would Poe Pick on Gisquet?

Henri-Joseph Gisquet took over as the Prefect of Police on October 15, 1831, replacing Louis Sebastien Saulnier, a man who lasted as prefect less than one month.[13] (The eight prefects prior to Gisquet had averaged less than six months each.) Gisquet would serve

---

13. It is quite possible that Gisquet's appointment was conjoined with Saulnier's redeployment. That is, the royalist Saulnier seems to have earned his September 1831 appointment as Prefect, due to his sophistical attack on the American government, claiming that a republic costs more to administer than a kingdom, published in the June 1831 *Revue Britannique* (a journal that he had founded in 1825). LaFayette then engaged James Fenimore Cooper to respond on the realities of governing in America. In turn, Saulnier's October 15 redeployment, taking point against LaFayette, Cooper, and General Simon Bernard in a series of public exchanges, became the infamous "Finances Controversy" in France's Chamber of Deputies.

Prefect Henri Joseph Gisquet

for the next five years. Two weeks later, on October 29, a shot was fired into Galois' room in prison, where all three prisoners were quietly preparing for a night's sleep. The shot was fired from a guard room. (It was never determined whether this was just an accidental discharge of a weapon, a deliberate attempt on Galois' life, or simply a warning shot, to send a message.) Galois and the other two were imprisoned in the dungeon for complaining about being fired upon. The other prisoners revolted, and temporarily took over the prison, securing Galois' release from the dungeon. Still alive, in November Galois was now officially charged by Gisquet for the July 14 demonstration. Found guilty as charged, he was scheduled for release on April 29, 1832.

Raspail described Galois in Sainte-Pélagie: "This slender, dignified child, whose brow is already creased, after only three years' study, with more than sixty years of the most profound meditation; in the name of science and virtue, let him live! In two years' time he will be Evariste Galois, the scientist! But the police do not want scientists of this caliber and temperament to exist." Raspail's *Reforme penitentiaire: Lettres sur les prisons de Paris* is the prime source for Galois' time in jail. Years later, in 1839, his publication of those letters

may have led to a renewed interest in Galois' case, either for Poe's 1841 "Murders in the Rue Morgue" or for Joseph Liouville's 1843 decision to edit and publish Galois' papers, or both. However, there is little doubt that it did provoke Gisquet, whose 1840 *Memoires* explained: "The government and the conspirators [Raspail's Society of the Friends of the People] were engaged in a relentless daily struggle ... I ordered the local branches dispersed as soon as they were founded, I had their papers confiscated, their members arrested."[14]

In January 1832, the trial of Raspail and fourteen other leaders of the Society of the Friends of the People took place. Galois was a witness for the defense. The jury found them not guilty, but the judge gave Raspail fifteen months in prison for statements he made during the trial. Raspail had threatened the King for demanding "fourteen million for living expenses of an impoverished France ... ." Raspail's attack reflected the then current debate in the Chamber of Deputies (January 16, 1832), known famously as the "Finances Controversy," in which Lafayette addressed the cost of a kingdom versus that of a republic. Briefly, Saulnier's *Revue Britannique*, months earlier—the same Saulnier who had been Prefect of Police just prior to Gisquet—had claimed that the American republic cost its citizens more than the French kingdom (hence, France should save money and choose a kingdom). This impelled Lafayette to request James Fenimore Cooper, then living in Paris, to provide Lafayette with an extensive report on America's economy, government, and finances for use in the debate.[15] Cooper's use of details of production and finances in the United States showed that a republic cost less per capita—basically because production per capita is higher.[16] Importantly, General Simon

---

14. A typical police report under Gisquet: "To the Minister of the Interior, Sir: I have just learned that Raspail ... has come to Lagny ... and has participated in an anti government dinner party. Raspail's apparent purpose is to learn about cereals and agriculture from peasants, farmers, and millers. The information seems necessary for the book he is writing; but since the trip might conceal a political purpose, I thought it my duty to keep you informed. Raspail will be discreetly watched during his stay ..."

15. Cooper's November 1831 letter to Lafayette, "On the Expenditure of the United States of America," used for Lafayette's testimony to the Chamber of Deputies.

16. Lafayette had requested Cooper's help in September 1831, but Cooper was finishing up *The Bravo*, his novel on Venetian methods—a work completely appropriate both for 1831 Paris and for his American readers. After completing it, Cooper worked with Lafayette on the "Finances Controversy" in November and December 1831. (Dumas' claim that Fenimore Cooper recommended Poe to him certainly dovetails with

Bernard, back from fourteen years in America, joined in the fray in coordination with Lafayette and Cooper. His relationship with West Point's Sylvanus Thayer and with Poe is developed below.

The Death of Galois

Galois' prison sentence was completed on April 29, 1832. One month later, on May 29, he spends the night writing to friends, informing them of a duel the next morning, and to his most trusted friend, Auguste Chevalier, providing a quick summary of his mathematical work. (This letter gained fame for the claim that Galois invented group theory in the hours prior to his shooting.) On May 31, he dies in the Cochin Hospital, a hospital for the indigent. Evidently, he had been found the previous day in the countryside by a peasant, with a bullet in his intestines. His brother, Alfred Galois, reported his last words were, "Don't cry. I need all my courage to die at twenty."

It is not known what details Evariste Galois communicated to his younger brother that last morning in the hospital, but Alfred insisted from the very first that his brother's death was the work of police agents. The next day, June 1, Galois' associates at the Society of the Friends of the People plan the funeral and the political demonstration. Gisquet has advance notice, raids the meeting, and arrests thirty of the leaders.[17] Despite all this, some two to three thousand show up for the funeral the next day and, despite Gisquet's insistence that they planned violence, they hold a funeral, not a violent demonstration.

The controversies over the shooting of Galois are well beyond the scope of this article. They involve, variously, police agents, a love interest, a duel with someone possibly with the initials "L.D.," and so on. The book-length treatment by Einstein's colleague, Leopold Infeld, *Whom the Gods Love*, develops the role of the extensive police-state control over the various characters.

What is of interest, rather, is what would have jumped out to Poe's Dupin: Gisquet's sole mention of

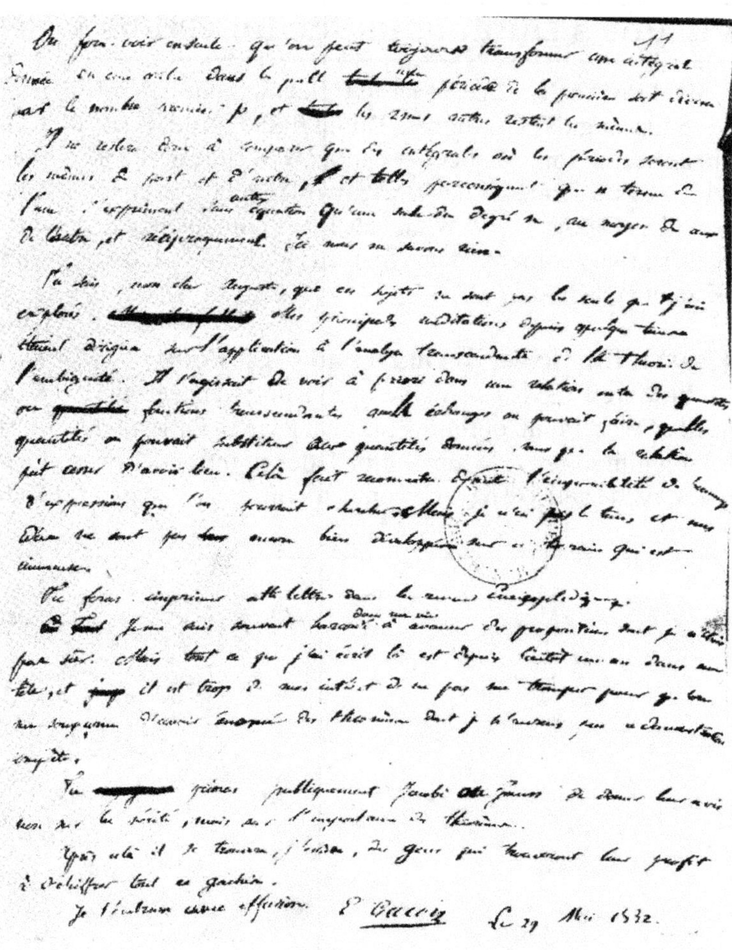

May 29, 1832: Galois' last page, to Auguste Chevalier: "Ask Jacobi or Gauss publicly to give their opinion, not as to the truth, but as to the importance of these theorems. Later there will be, I hope, some people who will find it to their advantage to decipher all this mess."

Galois occurs when he arrives in his *Memoires* at May 1831: "M. Galois, a fierce Republican, was killed in a duel by one of his friends." Otherwise Gisquet's version is that he had to raid the funeral planners because it was really a plot to start a violent revolution. And despite Gisquet's mass arrests, the only reason the 2-3,000 attendees didn't begin any trouble is because, at the last second, they heard that General Lamarque had just died of cholera, and so decided to delay their revolutionary rioting until Lamarque's funeral, three days later. As Dupin concludes "The Murders in the Rue Morgue," speaking of Police Prefect G____: "I like him especially for one master stroke of cant, by which he has attained his reputation for ingenuity. I mean the way he has 'of denying what is, and explaining what isn't.'"

Poe's 1831 request of Thayer for an introduction to Lafayette.)

17. Gisquet claims that he had put padlocks on the arranged meeting place, and that the group broke his padlocks. But, even if this were true, the point remains: Gisquet meant to physically prevent the meeting. He, again, explains what isn't and avoids what is.

Did Poe really have Evariste Galois in mind in creating his singular C. Auguste Dupin figure? And, if so, did he secure some justice for Galois? It is time now for a bit of Poe's side of the story, overlapping the same period as Galois' story. What was Poe's competency in "descriptive geometry" and what was his knowledge of Gisquet and Galois?

Thayer, the Ecole, Bernard and West Point

In March 1831, Poe wrote to Sylvanus Thayer, the head of West Point, outlining his plan to go to Paris, and asking him to provide him with a letter of introduction to Lafayette and to Thayer's contact(s) in Paris. Poe had studied at West Point from July 1830 to March 1831, where the leading mathematics text, prepared by the head of West Point's Department of Engineering, was Claudius Crozet's 1821 *A Treatise of Descriptive Geometry for the Use of Cadets of the U.S.M.A.* Thayer had recruited Crozet from the Ecole Polytechnique during his mission to Europe in 1815-1817, in preparation for becoming superintendent of West Point Academy in 1817.

Thayer had spent most of his two years there in Paris with members of the Ecole Polytechnique. It was a difficult and repressive period, as the restoration of the monarchy included the castration of the Ecole. Both Gaspard Monge and Lazare Carnot were forced out, and the Ecole was put under Cauchy's control. Thayer

Poe's letter to Gen. Sylvanus Thayer, March 1831: "Having no longer any ties which can bind me to my native country—no prospects—nor any friends—I intend by the first opportunity to proceed to Paris with the view of obtaining, thro' the interest of the Marquis de Lafayette, an appointment (if possible) in the Polish Army. In the event of the interference of France in behalf of Poland this may easily be effected—at all events it will be my only feasible plan of procedure. The object of this letter is respectfully to request that you will give me such assistance as may lie in your power in furtherance of my views. A certificate of "standing" in my class is all that I have any right to expect. Any thing farther—a letter to a friend in Paris—or to the Marquis—would be a kindness which I should never forget."

Fort Monroe, 1861

was led by Lafayette to former Ecole faculty, in particular, to his colleague, Gen. Simon Bernard, who, during 1816, would personally instruct Thayer in descriptive geometry. Lafayette wrote President Madison that General Bernard was the man to build fortifications for the United States all along the East Coast.[18] Bernard was appointed the head of the U.S. Corps of Engineers, and the Chief of Fortifications. The first fort that Bernard built for the United States was Ft. Monroe, in the port of Hampton and Norfolk, Virginia. Since Poe, prior to West Point, had been based there in 1829, he had the opportunity to study Bernard's real-life application of descriptive geometry.

Training at West Point

When, Poe arrived at West Point in June 1830, he promptly tested into the "first section," which included more advanced math topics (such as spherical geometry).[19] A fellow West Point student (the future Colonel) Allan Magruder, remembered Poe as having "a wonderful aptitude for math … ," only surpassed by his poetry and his command of French. Even though Poe had already decided to leave West Point, in the January 1831 math exam, he still placed 17th (out of 87 cadets). Poe was not a slacker in the subject.

How much of Crozet's *Descriptive Geometry* Poe was exposed to in his nine months there is unknown, but his Dupin character certainly evidences a command of the principles. Regardless, at the point of his arranged early departure from West Point, Poe thinks his best pathway is to pursue Thayer's French contacts around Lafayette.[20] It is also of note that Thayer's friend and instructor, Gen. Bernard, decided, no later than February 1831, to return to post-Restoration France, to become the head of the French Corps of Engineers. He arrived back in France in the Fall of 1831, and immediately joined in with Lafayette and Fenimore Cooper in their defense of the United States in the national deliberations over France's future. Such a development is not one that a sharp fellow, such as Poe, would likely have missed.

Alexandre Dumas tells the story that, in 1832, he and Poe investigated the murders in the Rue Morgue (though with the actual French neighborhood, St-Roch, given). He followed up his story with another reference to Poe's visit with him, embedded in a manuscript not written as fiction.[21] This fits in perfectly with Poe's

---

18. Around 1816, Bernard was banished from Restoration France. He rejected an offer from Czar Alexander I, preferring to come to the United States. After the British navy had savaged the U.S. East Coast during the War of 1812, Madison, learning the hard way, abandoned Jefferson's pre-war, "penny-wise and pound-foolish" policy of not providing such logistical capability.

19. In November 1830, Poe wrote home for math books, assumedly from his time at the University of Virginia. These included LaCroix's *Elements of Algebra* and Legendre's *Geometry*. The Charlottesville professor there who selected LaCroix for the students, one Charles Bonneycastle, belonged—according to Cajori—"to that coterie of English mathematicians of which Herschel, Peacock, Whewell, and others were members, and which introduced the Leibnizian notation … into Cambridge." They wanted to bring LaCroix's works into Cambridge University. See discussion of John Herschel's "The Principle of Pure Deism, in Opposition to the Dotage of the University" in *The New Dark Ages Conspiracy* by Carol White. Evidently, Bonneycastle did so for Charlottes-

ville.

20. Coincidentally, Poe forces himself out of West Point at the exact same time that Galois is forced out of the *Ecole normale*—the end of formal education for both of them.

21. Dumas' version was published in his own Naples newspaper in 1860-1861. A manuscript from 1864 surfaced in 1929, referencing

intent, as expressed in his letter to Thayer, and would account for his uncanny sense of a complicated political situation in France. However, putting aside the matter of Dumas' story, there is no doubt that over the next ten years, Poe displayed a healthy interest, an amazing acumen, and a strategic overview of the problems and developments in France—to a level that would make it even more amazing had he done all his work from America. A microcosm of this is enveloped in the matter of Poe's name of the poet-mathematician, "C. Auguste Dupin."

The 'Dupin' Riddle

There is no one actual figure with the name "C. Auguste Dupin" of whom Poe would have been aware. It is somewhat ironic that the infighting that goes on over the issue is such a strong example of the nitpicking methods of Vidocq and Gisquet. Poe's playfulness with the name is a much richer story. The central figure for Poe is that of Charles Dupin, whose 1819 lecture on Monge's *Descriptive Geometry* is excerpted above. Dupin was Monge's student at the Ecole Polytechnique,[22] and his studies significantly overlap those of Crozet, Bernard, and Thayer. Dupin's first major work, his 1813 *Developpements de geometrie*, was dedicated to Monge.

Dupin also had a political career, which featured attempts to eliminate illiteracy and to educate skilled labor in France, both for the purpose of enabling new scientific applications to radiate throughout production.[23] His electoral victory in 1827 was part of an up-

Edgar Allan Poe

surge of republicanism in France that would bring an end to the Restoration period. It is noteworthy that Charles Dupin and Gen. Bernard were fellow ministers (of Navy and of War, respectively) in the aborted November 1834 French government.[24] It would, perhaps, have been a semi-miracle if Dupin and Bernard had consolidated power in 1834, but regardless, the attempt was the sort of development that would easily have attracted Poe's attention.

There is also good evidence that Poe followed Charles Dupin's brother, André. He was the President of France's Chamber of Deputies from 1832 to 1840. André had a reputation as the legal defender of oppressed republicans during the Restoration period, most famously, of Marshal Ney. André attached himself to Louis-Philippe early on (1817) as the most sane possibility amongst the royal families. In 1830, upon the July Revolution, André initially became minister without portfolio in the first cabinet, that of Laffitte. André Dupin himself was a subject of Lomenie's *Sketches of Conspicuous Living Characters of France*, a work reviewed by Poe in the same April 1841 issue of *Graham's Magazine* in which C. Auguste Dupin first appeared.

Recall that Poe, in his 1844 "Purloined Letter," has the narrator bring up two brothers, the minister who knows mathematics, and the brother, a man of letters and poetry. The narrator doubts that the minister whom Dupin is tracking is really a poet-mathematician:

" 'But is this really the poet?' I asked. 'There are two brothers, I know; and both have attained reputation in

---

Poe's visit, but not written as a tale. It states that James Fenimore Cooper provided Poe an introduction to Dumas. Most telling, 1832 is the only year of Poe's writing career in which he sends nothing to a publisher. (The five stories published in 1832 were all given to his Philadelphia publisher in 1831.)

22. At the *Ecole*, Dupin constructed a specially designed structure for the invasion of Great Britain, which he and his fellow students christened the *Polytechnique*.

23. Dupin's 1827 election pamphlet, *Situation progressive des forces de la France depuis 1814,* was favorably noticed by Friedrich List and his Pennsylvania Society for the Encouragement of Manufactures. They

noted in particular the dirigist argument for uplifting the labor force. (Later, List's 1841 work, *The National System of Political Economy*, notes: "Men of the deepest insight into the condition of industry, such as Chaptal and Charles Dupin, had expressed themselves on the results of this system in the most unequivocal manner.")

24. The brawls over the cabinets of Louis-Philippe, the Citizen-King, were complicated—but Lafayette's 1830 deal with Louis-Philippe was perhaps the high point of the republican influence. After December 1830, most of the republican actions have a rear-guard quality.

letters. The Minister I believe has written learnedly on the Differential Calculus. He is a mathematician, and no poet.'

" 'You are mistaken; I know him well; he is both. As poet and mathematician, he would reason well; as mere mathematician, he could not have reasoned at all, and thus would have been at the mercy of the Prefect.' "

Here, Poe seems to use the reality of the actual Dupin brothers to further his case for the poet-mathematician. But, even further, Prefect Gisquet can defeat either of the actual Dupin brothers should they be merely poet or mathematician—a fair description as to where the actual brothers might have fallen short, and a pointed reminder as to why republicans need to hold themselves to higher standards.

How a Riddle Is Solved

So much for Charles and André Dupin. But Poe's Dupin is a "chevalier" named "C. Auguste Dupin." Certainly, the initial "C." could certainly be a nod toward Charles Dupin. However, no commentators deal with the obvious—the, as it were, "Purloined Letter"-type of clue of the remaining "Auguste" and "chevalier." There is an actual historical figure named Auguste Chevalier. We have met him. It is Galois' most loyal friend, the one spending the 1830s making clean copies of Galois' manuscripts and trying to make Galois' mathematical breakthroughs known to Gauss, Jacobi, and others.

How would Poe have known about Auguste Chevalier? It was not until 1843, two years after Poe's "Murders in the Rue Morgue," that Joseph Liouville went public with the Galois papers, given to him by Chevalier, in his announcement to the French Academy.[25] Poe might have read Galois' last letter, the one to Auguste Chevalier, as it was published in the September 1832 issue of the *Revue encyclopédique*. Further, Poe might have discussed matters with Auguste's close collaborator, his brother Michel Chevalier. Michel was in Baltimore at the same time as Poe, during Michel's 1833-

1835 study of American economics, government, and society on behalf of the French government.[26] However, the best evidence that Poe had Galois in mind was provided by a fascinating clue that Poe left, one that Dupin would have appreciated.

In 1846, a friend of Poe had brought up a current legal controversy in France, involving two different French translations of his "Murders in the Rue Morgue." Poe corrects his friend's assumption that the 1846 contretemps was the first introduction of Poe's name into France. He cites examples of prior responses in France to his writings, beginning as follows:

"The 'Murders in the R. M.' was spoken of in the Paris 'Charivari,' soon after the first issue of the tale in Graham's Mag: — April 1841."

The founder, publisher, and editor of *Le Charivari* was one Charles Philipon, a political prisoner along with Galois and Raspail at Sainte-Pélagie prison. Philipon's four-page daily was noted for its political cartoons. It, along with its predecessor (named *La Caricature*), was at the center of attacks upon Louis-Philippe, particularly because of his December 1830 betrayal of France. For example, Philipon's February 26, 1831 cartoon, entitled "Foam of July," had Louis-Philippe blowing bubbles representing the promises of the July Revolution. Philipon was prosecuted (and acquitted) just prior to the trial of the nineteen republican leaders. He was next prosecuted in November 1831. Evidently, at the trial itself, he presented his cartoon of "Louis-Philippe as a pear," which did the 1831 equivalent of "going viral."[27]

Poe, in simply invoking *Le Charivari*, speaks to anyone with ears what his introduction of Dupin is about. Clearly, Poe is aware of Philipon and his own history with Gisquet, and he chooses to redirect any discussion appropriately.

Various Poe experts assert, "Poe was simply mistaken. We've examined issues of *Le Charivari* in the period after Poe's work appeared, and we find nothing. Forget about it." But it seems that Dupin has struck again. The "Poe experts"—perhaps better addressed as

---

25. Joseph Liouville, Professor of Analysis and Mechanics at the Ecole Polytechnique, was the hero of the Galois manuscripts. He received them in 1842, worked through them, and in 1843, announced to the *Academie:* "These manuscripts have been entrusted to me by M. Auguste Chevalier" and need to be published, something he accomplished in 1846. Liouville was a moderate republican and political collaborator of Arago (another attendee at the 1831 celebration of Lafayette's Nineteen).

26. Michel makes reference to Robert Walsh of Philadelphia's *National Gazette* as one of the two best editors in America, a man with whom Poe had some dealings. Also, when Michel is in Baltimore, his reports refer to *Laffitte*, which might have been occasioned by discussions with Poe, but this is a pretty slender thread.

27. One unconfirmed story of Galois has him getting into trouble for a "Louis-Philippe/pear" drawing on his jail cell wall.

"Gisqueteers"—may search as relentlessly as Gisquet did in *The Purloined Letter*, for the words "Rue Morgue" in *Le Charivari*, but they will only explain *what isn't*.

But they deny what is. Poe's readers are treated to a rare form of causal reasoning, but one open to any child encouraged to develop a healthy relationship with the imagination, one that strengthens the power of the creative reason. And for this alone, Galois, Gisquet's "fierce republican," may yet gain his full measure of justice.

VII. Poe's Poet-Mathematician

Poe's playful introduction to his Dupin character posed the mental work of working backwards, to retrace how the freely moving imagination traversed its course. In pursuing such concentrated work, one is not guaranteed to capture the quarry every time—however it is an undeniably rich field, and the method indeed does work. In the spirit of Dupin's method, which he described in reverse as: "The larger links of the chain run thus—Chantilly, Orion, Dr. Nicholas, Epicurus, Stereotomy, the street stones . . . ," let us provide a brief example triggered not by street stones, but by Galois' work on the quintic. The reverse description runs as follows: "Immortality, loving God, human, golden mean, dodecahedron, family of five, unlimited fantasies and unlimited space, how to solve a fifth-power equation." And now, let's go off to the races:

Why would the solvability of equations involve descriptive geometry, and Platonic solids, in particular? How many regular solids are constructible in space? Oh, but aren't they as unlimited as my possible fantasy states? But why only five? What are the characteristics of this strange family of five? The dodecahedron is somehow "more equal of the equals," playing a generative role? What to make of its "golden mean" characteristic? Have we now encountered a theological/cosmological principle—that is, why should the Creator make man in the image of the Creator? Why choose to produce a "subgroup," that is, man, that somehow images the Creator? And, contrariwise, what

Philipon's "Louis-Philippe as a Pear," as it appeared in Le Charivari.

kind of a god would have created something not in its image?

Have we learned from this rapid fire "scientific" investigation that our God is a loving God, not a jealous one? Is this a beautiful idea, one that has the power to inspire—that is, one that may causally direct one's play towards loving future generations that we will never see? Has our unique personality been damaged by this "restriction" of our freedom, by having to deal with the problems of the world, into which we were created? Or does our mortal existence thereby touch immortality, finding true meaning in our having been created?

It may be a struggle for the mind to traverse the universe with any confidence in getting fruitful results, but it must be done, and it can be done. The power of mind that Poe analyzes at some length (in, e.g., his "Rationale of Verse") is not fundamentally different from that child, in the quiet evening hours, trying to retrace how its own imaginative steps were taken. Ideas take shape in the mind before they find their delineation in words.

Much is ventured about Galois, but in the "Gisquet"

fashion that Poe properly skewered. What is unmistakable about Galois, is that he clearly developed the "descriptive geometry" to raise the mind's analytic power. How is this different from what a true poet does? The struggle involved is in so loving one's fellow man, that one takes into one's heart—that one plunges into the history of man's passions as reflected in the development of language—both the noble passions and the destructive ones, and makes social a new pathway, one with the increased power to conquer previous encrustations of former progress.

We used Charles Dupin's quote on "descriptive geometry" to characterize Galois' method. Now, read it one last time, but with Poe's command of poetry in mind—where the "shapes of bodies in space" are now the "shapes of ideas in the mind (prior to verbalization)":

"One's mind must be especially trained in this general geometry. One must be able to represent the shapes of bodies in space, and to ideally combine these shapes by the sole power of imagination. The mind learns to see inwardly and with perfect clarity the individual lines and surfaces, and families of lines and surfaces; it acquires a feeling for the character of these families and individuals; it learns to see them combine them, and foresee the results of their intersections and of their more or less intimate contacts, etc. Thus the new geometry greatly strengthens the imagination; it teaches you how to grasp a vast collection of shapes quickly and precisely, to judge their similarities and differences and their relations of size and position ..."

Hence, Evariste Galois, Poe's poet-mathematician.

For Further Reading

Allen Salisbury, "Edgar Allan Poe: The Lost Soul of America," *Fidelio,* Spring/Summer 2006, https://www.schillerinstitute.org/fid_02-06/2006/061-2_Poe_Allen-S.html

Lyndon H. LaRouche, Jr., "The Day the Bomb Went Off in Chicago: A Short Story," *The Campaigner,* Vol. 14, No. 6, September 1981, http://www.wlym.com/archive/campaigner/8109.pdf This article provides LaRouche's reflections on Poe and his "C. Auguste Dupin."

Korea: Get the Tractors Rolling!

by Mike Billington

The following is adapted from a video presentation on LaRouchePAC TV on Aug. 15. See https://www.you-tube.com/watch?v=yTWwanhiHgM

Aug. 26—Headlines across the Western world over the past few weeks have been blaring that President Trump is about to nuke North Korea, and/or North Korea is about to nuke Guam. This is mostly hysterical nonsense. There is a grave danger that there could be a war provoked over North Korea, which would really not be targetting North Korea; but rather, targetting China. Or, to be more specific, targetting the very close, friendly relationship between President Trump and China's President Xi Jinping.

What I would like to do is put in historical context how this crisis, and one other perpetual crisis—the Palestinian-Israeli crisis—are intentionally created hotspots, created by the British and British intelligence networks within the United States and elsewhere. The only purpose for these seemingly unresolvable conflicts, is not to deal with the so-called regional crises in Korea or in the Middle East, but rather, to maintain a perpetual crisis scenario in which the British Empire can keep the world divided—and especially keep the world divided between East and West. The original set-up of the Israeli-Palestinian crisis, was from the very beginning intended to be a perpetual conflict, removing people from their homes, and creating territorial, religious and ethnic divisions which would be a basis for perpetual warfare by the British Empire. This is the whole idea of "divide and conquer"—sustaining a conflict which can be ignited anew whenever such a crisis is needed.

But behind the regional conflict, set up in order to

CasonVids/youtube

President Trump and President Xi Jinping at their April 6, 2017 meeting at Mar-a-Lago.

control the Middle East and so forth, was the idea that this would be a cockpit for war between the West and Russia, and with China. By creating this conflict between the Israelis and the Palestinians, you would effectively get all of the Western "free world" nations behind Israel, and all of the "dictatorial"—or "communist" in those days—forces from Russia and from China and elsewhere, supporting the Palestinians. Then you'd have no chance for the kind of policy Franklin Roosevelt was fighting for in World War II—namely, for the U.S. and Russia and China to work together to defeat fascism and end the British Empire—to end the destruction and looting of the Third World, and instead to bring American System methods to bear for the development of the formerly colonized nations in Africa, the Middle East, Asia, and so forth. So, this is *why* the Israeli-Palestinian conflict was created by the British Empire.

The same situation exists in Korea. The history of

how Korea got divided after World War II and how the Korean War got started—I won't try to go into all of that. But the British wanted to keep that division permanent; they didn't want peace between North and South Korea. They wanted to keep a perpetual crisis there which would keep the United States and the Europeans on the side of South Korea, and the Chinese and the Russians on the side of North Korea; and thereby prevent any chance for the U.S., Russia and China to come together behind a development perspective which would counter the power of the British Empire.

I want to go through a couple of historical facts about this situation. Not the origin of the crisis, but something that developed in the 1990s which I think will provide a very clear flavor of how this works.

In 1993, the Oslo Accords were signed between the Israelis and the Palestinians, with Bill Clinton, then the President of the United States, as the primary sponsor. The agreement was worked out in Oslo, with Russian collaboration, but essentially in secret—in particular, in secret from the British. The British were not involved; they were kept out of the negotiations, for very good reasons. When Bill Clinton came into office, he said that the special relationship America would have under his leadership would be with Germany, not with the UK. That's why he was eventually watergated and impeached. It wasn't Monica Lewinsky—she was used in order to bring him down for the crime of failing to follow dictates from Britain.

This is why Lyndon LaRouche began to give his qualified support to President Bill Clinton, who was breaking the British domination of U.S. policy-making after the death of FDR, and even more so after the assassination of JFK. This was quite the opposite of what Hillary Clinton became later on—a complete tool of the British, advocating confrontation and war with Russia and with China.

So at that time, Bill Clinton orchestrated this potential peace agreement in the Middle East. The Oslo

Israeli Prime Minister Yitzhak Rabin (left), PLO Chairman Yasser Arafat (right), and U.S. President Bill Clinton at the Oslo Accord signing ceremony in Washington D.C., September 1993.

Accord was really quite profound; it led to Israeli Prime Minister Rabin and PLO leader Arafat coming to Washington, shaking hands with Bill Clinton at the White House, and committing themselves to a long-term policy for peace in the Middle East. What was most important about the Oslo Accord was not just that the Israelis were going to remove some of their troops from Gaza and from some of the West Bank, and that the Palestinians were going to recognize Israel's existence and so forth. That was important, but the real importance was something they called the Palestine-Israel Committee for Economic Cooperation. They were going to work together for the development of the Middle East, and the Palestinian territories in particular. Mr. LaRouche at that time said—immediately, I remember clearly the day when the Oslo Accord was announced—within minutes, Mr. LaRouche said "Get the tractors rolling! Get the development process going, and don't let the World Bank or the IMF anywhere near this process, or the tractors will never roll."

LaRouche argued that you must have a development process in place which locates the actual interests of both sides of this conflict; a development process which would put the skilled Palestinian workers to work, building especially water projects, with scientists from Israel and experienced Israeli corporations which would be able to develop the water, the energy, the transportation, and all the infrastructure needed for that region to develop, to resolve the poverty on the Palestinian side, and bring Israelis and Palestinians together in a collaborative process.

Well, the exact opposite happened. Rabin was killed by the right-wing British assets within Israel, and the situation rapidly unravelled. But most important, again, the reason it didn't work, was because they put the World Bank in charge of overseeing the development process; which meant there was not going to be any development. The World Bank's argument was that "Well, we can't expect the private sector to come in here and invest if there's not peace. We have to have peace first, then we can have development." LaRouche insisted that the exact opposite was the case. Get the development process rolling, and then you have a basis on which a political settlement can actually make sense and be lived up to.

So, what was the British purpose? The purpose, as I said, was to keep the division between the United States and Russia; which is why the British moved in to crush Oslo, including the killing of Israel's greatest leader—Yitzhak Rabin.

Now, look at the Korea situation; it's really precisely the same. The Oslo Accord was in 1993. In 1994, just one year later, Bill Clinton organized something called the "Agreed Framework" regarding North Korea. We were on the brink of war in 1992-93 with North Korea, over nuclear weapons. They had built a nuclear power plant that was producing weapons-grade material, at the Yongbyon nuclear complex, and we were insisting that they stop; and they said no. But through a process—Jimmy Carter got involved somewhat on behalf of Clinton—but primarily it was Clinton and his Defense Secretary William Perry—who is still today the most sensible mind on the whole Korea situation—who moved in and said, "Let's actually guarantee North Korea's energy and their security, in exchange for their giving up any program for producing nuclear weapons." And it worked! They signed. Kim Jong-il signed; and when he died, his son signed. The "Agreed Framework" worked. They shut down the Yongbyon nuclear plant in exchange for us building them another nuclear plant that didn't produce weapons-grade material, providing them with oil, and providing a framework toward having a peace agreement between the United States and North Korea. We're still officially at war with North Korea ever since the Korean War, because there was only an armistice, not a peace agreement.

So, the process was taking place. There were fits and

World Economic Forum/swissimage.ch/Remy Steinegger

Former Vice President Dick Cheney.

starts, but during the entire Clinton Administration this moved forward; the U.S. and South Korea began building the nuclear plant; there were regular negotiations; and UN inspectors were brought in with North Korea's concurrence. Things were moving.

Then, boom! Bush and Cheney came in; the neo-cons took over—Dick Cheney in particular. Even though the Secretary of State, Colin Powell, said, as soon as he came in, "We are going to continue with the Agreed Framework; we are going to continue this process which is working to bring peace to the Korean peninsula"—Cheney said, "Like Hell!" and squashed it, and accused the North Koreans of cheating. The whole thing was scrapped. There was an effort by the South Koreans, under Kim Daejung, and the Chinese and the Russians to keep the process going with what they called the "Six Party Talks," with Japan and the United States. But the problem was, they didn't really have the United States supporting this process; it was Bush and Cheney. Theirs was a neo-con policy—geopolitics. They quickly undermined the deal, saying the North Koreans were cheating, and the whole process got scrapped. The North then threw the UN out and began building nuclear weapons. It didn't help when they saw what happened to Iraq when they gave up their nuclear weapons program, and Bush and Cheney proceeded to bomb them back to the stone age, kill their leader, dismantle their army, and turn the country over to warring terrorist factions.

When you move toward establishing peace on a sensible basis, as in these two crucial hotspots, the British and their assets in the U.S. move in immediately to crush it. Why? Because they don't want peace. Do they like war? Yes, local "surrogate" wars—but even global war is viewed as acceptable, if it's necessary to prevent the U.S. coming together with Russia and China, which would threaten the British Empire's control through its control of the world financial system, its control of trade, and so forth.

Now the whole Western financial system is in a state of general breakdown. That is, in a certain sense, an advantage, to show to the American population why this anti-Russia, anti-China hysteria has to end. That we have to do what Trump wants to do, which is to bring the U.S. into line with the New Silk Road of China, and to work with Russia on countering the terrorist scourge; and most important, to bring back the American System here, based historically on the Hamiltonian policies of our Founding Fathers, but in paticular on what Roosevelt did in countering fascism—as we have to counter terrorism today—through collaboration among Russia, China, and the United States.

So, this is what is now taking place in Korea. There is reason for optimism; because very high-level diplomacy is taking place. The foreign minister of North Korea met with both the Chinese and Russian foreign ministers in Manila just last week. And we now know that President Trump has reinitiated back channel discussions through his envoy to North Korea, Joseph Yun, with the North Korean ambassador to the United Nations in New York.

So while there's a lot of fire in the news, in the headlines, and accusations flying back and forth, very serious diplomacy is taking place along the lines of the kind of policy that Mr. and Mrs. LaRouche have fought for throughout these last 50 years; which is to get a development process going which addresses the common aims, the common needs of all nations and all peoples. Then these political problems—caused and orchestrated by the British Empire—can be brought to an end. In other words, there's no reason for the Korean crisis or for the Middle East crisis to exist any longer. They only exist in order to maintain the British division of the world into East versus West. If President Trump succeeds in bringing those nations together for development along the LaRouche principles, then there's no cause for these crises, and they can be resolved almost overnight.

That's where we stand. This is a fight which can and must be won; but it's one that, in fact, is in keeping with the needs of the human race at a moment of great crisis for our species.